My Soul to Keep

My Soul to Keep

TOOLS FOR STAYING IN
A CHANGING CHURCH

CAROL BONOMO

NEW YORK • LONDON

2004

The Continuum International Publishing Group Inc
15 East 26 Street, New York, NY 10017

The Continuum International Publishing Group Ltd
The Tower Building, 11 York Road, London SE1 7NX

www.continuumbooks.com

Copyright © 2004 by Carol Bonomo
www.carolbonomo.net

All rights reserved. No part of this book may be reproduced, stored
in a retrieval system, or transmitted, in any form or by any means,
electronic, mechanical, photocopying, recording, or otherwise,
without the written permission of the publishers.

Printed in the United States of America

Library of Congress Cataloging-in-Publication Data
Bonomo, Carol, 1952-
   My soul to keep : tools for staying in a changing church /
by Carol Bonomo.
     p. cm.
   Includes bibliographical references and index.
   ISBN 0-8264-1640-3 (pbk. : alk. paper)
   1. Spiritual life – Catholic Church.   I. Title.
BX2350.3.B65 2004
248.4′82 – dc22

                             2004012310

For Father Don Coleman
who, on June 22, 2004,
celebrated thirty years as a priest.

His homilies at the 5:30 p.m. Mass
eventually disturbed my reading so much
that I put down my book
and began to listen.

Contents

Prologue

"Dear Richard," I e-mail my banjo-playing buddy, "if I don't write any faster, there either won't be interest on the subject of staying Catholic in a time of change, or else I'll be sitting with the Quakers and *I* won't be interested.

"Why don't you study stability through your ukulele practice?" he sends back. "Why bother with that church thing at all?"

"Well, my church has the best religious art I've ever seen. It's only three miles from my house, and they keep the air-conditioning on high in the summer. Things like that keep me in the faith sometimes."

"Of course," he answers. "First things first."

Acknowledgments

In Galatians 6:4–5, Paul writes, "Each one must examine his own work, and then he will have reason to boast with regard to himself alone, and not with regard to someone else; for each will bear his own load."

I did not bear the load of this book alone, and so have no cause to boast. Heartfelt thanks to Nancy Fitzgerald of Morehouse Publishing, who originally read this manuscript and sent it (and me) along to Continuum, but maintained the steady flow of e-mail communication so I wouldn't feel adrift in a new land.

Thanks also to Frank Oveis, senior editor at Continuum, for his effort and enthusiasm in turning this manuscript into a book.

Father Ron Chochol of St. Stephen Protomartyr Parish in St. Louis, Missouri, must be sick of the sound of my written voice by now, but kindly and carefully reviewed my tools of stability with me for soundness and appropriateness. It was our e-mail conversations back and forth that initially triggered the idea of this book.

Once again, Richard Riehl, banjo player extraordinaire, painstakingly reviewed the manuscript and laughed hysterically at everything he thought was "self-indulgent nonsense" until I took it out. At least I hope I did. Paige Jennings, my co-worker, was game for brainstorming anything.

Felix, as always, is my rock and support. The older we grow together, the more we blend into something resembling the sacrament of marriage.

And Blessed Joanna Mary, my Benedictine patron, stood patiently in the background and never laughed once, even when I was trying to be funny.

CAROL JOANNA MARY BONOMO ·
www.carolbonomo.net

ONE

Tools of the Trade

W HEN WE RAN AWAY from home as adults, we finally
did it right. When we were kids trying to run away,
it was usually a matter of packing a few treasures — if our
desperation or rage allowed us the time to pack at all — and
then embarking on a trip that lasted as long as our legs, imagination, courage, or anger would take us. For most of us, that
meant to the edge of the driveway or to the turn in the road
where our house was no longer visible to us. Once we realized
it was our *home* we were leaving, and not just the circumstances that drove us, we usually called a halt to the runaway
adventure and slunk back home to our familiar landscape.

As adults, it wasn't that we had more courage or strength,
only more options. We could fly or drive away before anybody
had time to know we had left. And we knew the secret about
running away from home: it gets easier with practice. What we
didn't seem to learn, however, was that no matter how little
you pack, you will always find a stowaway in your bags — the
troubles you thought were left behind. Once you lose sight of
home, you can easily move from runaway to lost.

I finally ran away from home when I was twenty-five years
old. I'd had a disastrous early marriage, a terrible job in one of
the dying industrial mills of New England, and I'd just flunked
out of adult religious education class. The final straw came

when my cat, Mozart, had to be put to sleep for a urinary blockage that was killing him painfully. I could handle a lot of stuff, but the loss of my cat was the end of my old life. I packed my clothes and half of the music collection and took a Greyhound bus to Boston to look for a new job and a new life.

It was easy enough to do. There were hundreds — maybe thousands — of people like me pouring into the Boston–Cambridge area every year just before Labor Day. Many were new or continuing students at the more than one hundred colleges and universities wedged along the Charles River. Many others were family members of graduate students setting up temporary homes during the course of study. And some were runaways like me, leaving home to look for ourselves. A secretarial job at one of those colleges or universities was like waitressing work in Hollywood — it paid the rent and the therapy while we were finding ourselves or being discovered.

I was one of five new secretaries hired in the Department of Chemistry at MIT that month. The academic enterprise needed a lot of foot soldiers, and these weren't career positions, so turnover was high every year. "Get to know each other," the cheerful administrative officer for the department told the five of us at orientation. "This is your peer group. It will be easier and less lonely if you come together as a group."

We did not, of course. We had nothing in common but a start date and the fact that we had found this particular institution when we ran away from home. Maybe we could no longer see our house from where we stood — one Californian, one midwesterner, two New Englanders, and one silent spouse of a Pakistani graduate student — but that didn't make *this* home either, dammit. Or make us suddenly kin.

But the Californian pulled us together two months after we began work, in what almost resembled a family council.

Four of us showed up after work to drink coffee at the Muddy Charles Pub and to discuss the fifth member of this peer group, a midwestern transplant named Jill.

She had converted to Islam. When I met Jill at orientation, she was rabbity-pale with watery blue eyes and freckly-white skin. Her hair was the color that we used to call dishwater blonde. She was one of those women who seemed to disappear behind her glasses. Her best feature was the melancholy sweetness of her brief little smiles. At orientation, she, more than any of us, looked like a lost, terrified puppy.

Now she was found, and she began dressing like she'd found herself at the bottom of a rummage sale. She came to work in layers and layers of mismatched, rumpled, threadbare long skirts and men's shirts under ratty sweaters with pulls in their stitching. She wore hair coverings made of different pieces of fabric that looked like rags to me. Only her watery blue eyes behind the horn-rimmed glasses remained familiar — and the sweet smile. When I saw her in the halls and waved or said hello nowadays, she smiled more now than when she first arrived. She wasn't hiding behind her glasses anymore.

"Jill's converted to Islam," said the Californian, when the four of us were seated. It was America in 1978. We were moderately sophisticated in Cambridge — we knew Muslims existed. We thought they existed somewhere else though, not here among university secretaries. We didn't know anybody who converted to Islam. We didn't know you *could* convert to Islam.

"She says she's very happy now," said the Pakistani secretary crisply. "I spoke with her several times. She wanted to know about religious practices in Pakistan and India. She said she found what she's been looking for."

We processed this information doubtfully. Maybe we were looking and lost too, but did the answers that came result in making you dress like *that*?

"Americans!" the Pakistani woman continued with a laugh. "Everything here is like hide-and-seek games, no focus, and nothing about who you are, always about who you will be. It's not like this where I come from, but I hope for Jill's sake, she found what was lost."

She finished the juice she was sipping and stood up. "Child care," she said apologetically. "I have to leave."

The three of us waited politely until she was safely gone. She was *different* from us, from a different country, but also married and a mother. Jill was like us when she came here, and then she went and got really different. We needed to know and understand the difference or else, we feared, it could happen to us. We'd wake up one morning wanting to wear rags over our hair, bowing and praying and saying how happy we were.

Wisely, we concluded that Jill was lonely and isolated, and had just reached out to whoever had befriended her and made her whole. It was that simple, and therefore didn't have to happen to us.

"But Islam!" cried the Californian as we finished our discussion. "How could she *do* that with the way they treat women?"

It was a depressing thought. I used it as the reason to get drunk alone in my studio apartment that night. Sometimes it was good to get drunk with righteousness and wine, although most nights I didn't have a reason at all. That worked, too.

That was nearly twenty years ago. Since then, I've become a Californian, a Roman Catholic, a Benedictine oblate (a lay-person affiliated with a monastic community living under a rule of life), a former drunk, a lobbyist by profession, a writer, and an artist.

It was as writer/author that I stood in front of a large and enthusiastic audience at the Episcopal cathedral one Sunday morning. There are readings by authors where the author reads and the audience listens. And then there are other readings that are dances between author and audience. This one was a dance, and we oohed and aahed each other's moves in turn. The questions were thoughtful and thought-provoking, and none of us wanted the dance to end. Finally, the canon said, "One more question before we need to get ready for the next service, yes?"

The woman waving her hand for attention looked apologetic and confused as she began. "I've loved the reading, and I've enjoyed this morning so much, and I bought the book, so don't get me wrong..."

The music paused. The dancers waited.

"...you said you were brought up an Episcopalian?"

"Yes."

"Well then, what I don't understand is: why would you ever convert to Catholicism? The way they treat women?"

Why indeed. Even as she waited, so perplexed, so wanting to know how her church had "failed" and Catholicism — of all weird women-crunching sects! — had succeeded with me, even as they all waited, the decades rolled back to Jill and our horror at her newfound comfort and her sweet smile.

"Well, I didn't convert *because* of the church's stance on women..." I began.

It got a laugh and it got me off the hook as we broke up. Which was a good thing, because if the next question had been, "What's the Catholic Church's stance on women?" I'd have been sunk.

Why Catholic? Well, why not? Born Catholics have a ready-made answer, although, "because I was born this way" is a pretty passive response. But this book isn't written because some of us were "born this way" and therefore "stay this way." The church of the born-Catholic is in fast-forward change mode, and has been for forty years. And pity the converts who *think* they know what they are converting to (or why) — until the changes or controversies flare up again.

I have yet to find a Catholic — born or self-selected — who answers the *why* Catholic question with its social justice policies or even with its theology. I have a former neighbor who "goes Catholic" — not the same as "being" Catholic for sure, but close enough in her mind — because the Catholic Church near her has a better program for widows than any other denomination, and *her* denomination, right now, is widow. I know converts who are so because of marriages and children, and I know cradle Catholics who stay Catholic, not because of what it means, or "how they treat women," but because they've got the habit of being Catholic, with or without faith.

Here we are, anyway, however we got here. The Catholic churches in southern California are packed at masses in languages that range from English to Spanish to Samoan to Tagalog to Vietnamese. We're here — but how do we *stay* here in this changing church and troubled religious history? Even cradle Catholics, with a churchgoing habit to feed, may find themselves stuck on the how-to part and become willing to hear somebody else's tools of the trade.

The church itself is not the immovable font of holiness and righteousness that an older generation once found it to be. As one astute commentator of the church writes:

... older Catholics have grown accustomed to the idea
of changes in practices that they never expected would
be altered — Mass in Latin, no meat on Friday, no han-
dling of the consecrated host — and younger Catholics
have never been inculcated with the idea of a church
beyond change.[1]

Some of the change has been dramatic, worship-altering
change — the priest facing you and speaking your language,
for example. But even that change has now had generations
behind it. Cradle Catholics in their mid-to-late thirties, or
converts during the last thirty years, have known nothing else.
Some of the changes are smaller and more annoying. Think
of the effect of a mosquito in your bedroom. If the bishops
update their translation of the Bible one more time, where
all the "wills" become "shalls," for example, I will scream.
If there's another edict about genuflecting before receiving
Communion versus a bow of the head, I will trip over the
next confused individual in line. This just isn't change where
most Catholics live.

In a morning reflection practice that the monks call *lec-
tio divina* (sacred reading), I sat with a verse from the book
of Psalms that was richly textured and rhythmic — *Fresh and
green are the pastures where he gives me repose, near restful waters
he leads me.*[2] The good thing about these new biblical translations, I thought, is that they take me along fresh roads of
exploration and reflection that the old, familiar translations
will not. I can't read the old, beloved King James Version of
Isaiah, for instance, because the music from Handel's *Messiah*
gets stuck in my head, and the mental chorus crowds out any
attempt at reflection. The bad news, however, is that *nothing* is familiar anymore. We end up as people in an ancient

religious tradition that no longer has either the ancient or the
traditional left. And in this translation of the Psalms I was reflecting on, the most beloved of psalms, the Twenty-third, was
renumbered more authentically to Psalm 22. Who knows that
this pretty verse I am reading was once remembered and wept
over at funerals? — *He makes me to lie down in green pastures;*
he leads me beside still waters.[3]

I used several dozen biblical citations in a book I wrote,
careful to utilize an official Catholic translation of the Bible
for my work. Alas, when the time came to request permission to use the verses, I learned that my quotes were from
the 1978 edition of the *New American Bible.* Regretfully, the
bishops were only authorizing citations using the 1986 or later
editions. I went back to see how much the translation change
would affect my wording. Genesis 28:21, the first reference of
many, showed me what the bishops had been up to: *Surely,*
the Lord is in this place; and I did not know it, had now become:
Surely the Lord is in this spot; and I did not know it.[4]

"Don't bishops have anything better to do these days?" I
complained to my mother, who is an Episcopalian and can't
understand why I wanted to convert either, but is glad I have
something, even if it is a Catholic something.

"They do important work that you know is important, and
important work you *don't* know is important," she said. "Try
not to second-guess the bishops or you'll make yourself crazy
and leave."

"It's too late. I *am* second-guessing, and they *are* making
me crazy, and I'm packing my bags too."

"Well, you have to stick with something," she said. This
was stunningly Benedictine wisdom that left me all sullen and
sulky and muttering, "Well, I wish the *church* would follow
that advice too!"

What I have needed for the tough times, the boring spots, the crazy-making headlines, are tools I can pull out to anchor myself in the church. Faith in God is usually not my problem. Faith in the rest of us, in the life of the church, can be.

In the sixth century, St. Benedict wrote a little book — barely larger than a fat pamphlet — on living together and making the life together holy. Benedictine monks and nuns vow to follow his way of life as laid out in this Rule of St. Benedict. So do laypeople like me, who become Benedict's "prayer friends" through their affiliation with a Benedictine monastery.

One of the chapters in Benedict's Rule is called "The Tools of Good Works." This chapter is nothing more — or less! — than a roundup of seventy-two commandments or Gospel injunctions, such as feed the hungry, clothe the naked, etc. Benedict includes the tools early in his little how-to book because, as my father would say, you never know when you're going to need the right tool for the right job, so it's best to keep them handy. My father would add that you can never have enough tools. My father's love of tools was reflected in his fully stocked toolbox ready to fix life's challenges. He would have liked Benedict's philosophy.

Benedict kept a fully stocked tool kit in his Rule too, making sure his monks were equally well prepared for their quest to live the holy life together.

Maybe I have tools, like Benedict or my father did, that keep me Catholic — prayer tools and traditions that bind me and remind me of the faith and the faces of the faithful. As a collage artist, I've become experienced at taking the bits and pieces of other works and other lives — pieces of books and poems, snapshots, colored fabric, magazine images — and reassembling them into a new work. In some way, that might be what my faith toolbox looks like — fragments of an older church culture overlaid on the shiny magazine surface of today, creating a lived life of faith that stays in a church of change.

I don't have every tool in my kit yet. The Catholic Church, its history, its practices, and its structures, requires many lifetimes of study. And I am not particularly the studious type. What I *am* is an ordinary member of those supersized congregations, who wants a meaningful life of faith, who would like to stay within that faith because she really doesn't know where else to go, and — if it isn't too much trouble, God? — would like to have some *fun* in this walk of faith with God. Do we get to dance, too? Is that too much to ask?

Here is my grab bag of Catholic tools of the moment. Some, like Mary, the Eucharist, the Rule of St. Benedict, and the Divine Office, are ancient in origin, although newly dressed in today's clothes. Others, like the rosary, novenas, the practice of adoration, and celebration of the holy days of obligation, flourished in the European Middle Ages. They became firmly entrenched in the American Catholic culture through the 1950s, but have nearly disappeared in today's practice. Finally, what I call "Broken Heart" — the heart of the church shown by the love of its members for each other — is both old and new, timeless and changing, exactly as the church is itself.

All of them are my tools for living a Catholic life. I've run away from home enough times to become an expert. These tools are for helping me stay.

TWO

Hail Mary

THE RITE OF CHRISTIAN INITIATION OF ADULTS — RCIA — begins in early fall at my church, just as school starts. There are a few times each year when resolve seizes us with the desire to *do*, to *be*, to *become*. New Year's Eve ushers in such resolve, sometimes birthdays ending in zeros, and frequently the beginning of the school year.

Some of the best parts of our educational experience, like learning new things, are wasted on our youthful years. When we're kids, school is about socializing and accessorizing, with droning teachers as background noise to be filtered out.

As we grow older and learn what we missed the first time through, the back-to-school ads tug at our nostalgia and missed opportunities. Some of us begin again — resolve to learn new computer skills, prepare for that better job, become "bigger, better, stronger" as the ads for my fitness center say at that time of year.

It is a time conducive to new beginnings. Give the house its fall cleaning. Plant the bulbs so you can have the early spring blooms you wished for too late last year. Take the photography class for enrichment. Sign up for the college introductory History of Western Civ course to see if you've got what it takes to get that degree while you're also working and raising a family. Become a Roman Catholic.

Huh? How did *that* slip in there?

My church's RCIA cranks up every year just before the kids go back to school, a start that seems more timed for school-supply ads than for anything in the church's liturgical year. It begins for us in the late middle of that great swath of time the church calls "ordinary time." For the church, the First Sunday of Advent is the beginning of its new year, and that doesn't begin until after Thanksgiving. For the RCIA class of the last year, "graduation" came at the Great Easter Vigil or perhaps sometime during Pentecost. But that class is all gone now, scattered into the weeks of ordinary time that follow Pentecost.

The church bulletin announced each week in August that RCIA would begin soon. If you are ready to join the church, "fully partake" of its sacramental offerings, or just want to know more about the faith you dragged into your adulthood maybe without too much thought, come in and find out. Light refreshments will be served. And if you don't have a sponsor to come with you, we'll have extras to share!

I showed up with my next-door neighbor that steamy August night, listening to words as meaningless to me that night as school lessons when I was in sixth grade. But when the paper came around to sign up, I never hesitated. I rarely hesitate when I sign up for things, rarely read the job description or list of requirements, if available. Becoming a Catholic was no exception. If I *knew* what lay ahead of me, I'd probably never go forward with any resolve. And this particular resolve had been waiting for me for nearly ten years.

"Let's begin at the beginning," said Deacon John to the twenty or so of us who came back for instruction two weeks after the social hour kickoff to RCIA. Our sponsors and a few extras hovered in straight-back school chairs behind us while we formed a circle around Deacon John.

"Why are we here?" he asked gently.

We began around the circle, twenty adults ranging in age from twenty-five to fifty, all white, successful-looking people sitting on little chairs, taking the first little step to a big undertaking.

"I married a Catholic, my children are Catholic, and I want to join them on Sunday mornings..."

"My kids are asking questions, and I don't have answers..."

"I'm engaged to a person who's Catholic..."

"I want to set a good example for my kids..."

"I was baptized and made First Communion, but in my teens I drifted away...."

Variations of those themes went around the circle, confirming what researchers have found to be true — that most people who convert to Catholicism do so largely because of interchurch marriage and the children who follow.[1] I wasn't sure what I would say when it was my turn. Felix is a seeker without affiliation, which is an interfaith marriage of a different sort. We married in an Episcopal church and have no children together.

When it was my turn, I went with the early version of the truth. "I've wanted to be Catholic my whole life. When I was a kid, I used to play nun with my sister, which made my Protestant grandmother mad. It just happens that I was born to parents who weren't Catholic, so now I'm fixing that."

Everybody laughed. "Welcome home," said Deacon John softly.

I had neatly evaded the real questions he posed: *Why now? Why at all?*

Months later, the catechumate class took a field trip to
a large downtown church where the bishop would hold the
Rite of Election. We weren't terribly well prepared for what
was happening, and it was happening to thousands of us in
an unfamiliar church where cantors and lectors traded off
between English and Spanish, thus losing a large part of par-
ticipant understanding with each change of language. When
the ceremony was finally over, we trundled back into our two
vans to ride back to the familiar. No one spoke much, but
finally the real-estate agent in our group trying to catch up to
her kids' hard questions turned to me and said, "So why are
you *really* doing this?"

Everybody in the van waited. I tried to think of the proper
terminology or titles to use, and finally said, "It's Hail Mary."

"The Blessed Mother? You are becoming Catholic for her?"

"Yes. For her. It's complicated."

Nobody in the van asked for the complicated details, which
was good because I don't know that I could have explained
how this was my thank-you note, my own Magnificat, after
all these years. They would have thought me crazy or maybe
drunk. *They have had too much wine,* as the devout ones said
of the apostles and possibly Mary as they were filled with
the Holy Spirit and rushed out to speak a babble of foreign
tongues on Pentecost.[2] I didn't even quite know how to refer
to the Mother of God, and probably sounded like I was dissing
her by using a common name without titles or glory.

Brought up in the late 1960s American Protestant tradition, I could sum up my knowledge of Mary the way most of
my Protestant friends did: Catholics prayed to Mary. (Why
would they do that?) We were not Catholic. (We were not
even friends with Catholic kids. They had big families and
strange, Mediterranean taste in food, and odd, exotic customs,

involving candles, statues, and Mary!) We prayed straight to
God — if we prayed at all. In that age and culture, prayer was
a Sunday thing that got in the way of the good music.

My confusion would be understandable. Mary, the Mother
of Jesus, probably called Miriam in her lifetime (meaning
myrrh) is known in the Bible for her acceptance of the call
to bear God's Son and for her beautiful song of divine praise,
the Magnificat:

> *My soul proclaims the greatness of the Lord;*
> *My spirit rejoices in God my savior.*
> *For he has looked upon his handmaid's lowliness* . . .[3]

She makes a few more cameo appearances — finding Jesus
in the Temple, asking for a miracle at a wedding in Cana, asking after Jesus during his teaching ministry, being present at his
Crucifixion. But legend, dogma, theology, and apparitions have
rendered her cult large and bewilderingly multifaceted, even to
those who are currently petitioning her cause as co-redeemer
(with Jesus) of the world to be her new official job description.

What do I call her? Her titles — there are over 6,000 Marian titles gathered up on one Web site alone[4] — come from
traditions originating in geography, human activity, needs,
events related to our salvation, theological titles, and devotional practices. Few of these titles have been made official by
church decree, although some (Our Lady of Lourdes, Most
Holy Name of Mary) are used in the cycle of liturgical feasts.
On rare, lovely Saturday nights when I participate in the com-
pline service at the local Benedictine abbey of my affiliation,
just when you think that the monks and I are finally done
praying for the day, instead of marching off to bed, they file
devoutly to the altar of Our Lady of Einsiedeln (Our Lady of
the Hermits). There, the cantor leads and the monks respond

to a haunting devotion called the Litany of Loreto, which is
nearly entirely composed of invocations or titles:

> V. Holy Mary.
> R. Pray for us.
>
> V. Holy Mother of God.
> R. Pray for us.
> ...
> Mother of Christ, Mother of Divine Grace ...
> Mother most amiable ...
> Virgin most faithful ...
> Mirror of justice ...
> Seat of wisdom ...
> Mystical rose ...
> Ark of the covenant ...
> Morning star ...
> Consolation of the afflicted ...
> Queen of martyrs ...
> Queen of the most holy Rosary ...
>
> R. Have mercy on us.[5]

All of these titles, glory, prayers, and artist renderings have
turned the mother of Jesus into her most-honored status over
the centuries. And uncovering even a bit of this intense
tradition was nearly culture shock to me.

Mary is everything we need or desire her to be if I just look
at her titles again: good counsel, lady of refuge, comforter of
the afflicted when we suffer; most powerful, most renowned,
and most venerable when we are on the side of the angels.

The titles most familiar revolve around what might, in our
times, be reduced to sexual commentary: *virgin*. It seems odd
that this woman — so unique in our salvation history, so

honored since — is represented, glorified, or dismissed by a
word that nowadays only holds sexual connotations. In ancient times, virginity described a state of independence or
autonomy — not a common situation for women then or in
most history since. Queen Elizabeth I, the Virgin Queen, used
the title in this capacity. When used to describe Mary, it
means, among other things, that she said "yes" to God in
her own freedom, acting independently of any coercion or
influence. Her Magnificat (*My soul proclaims the greatness of
the Lord; my spirit rejoices in God my savior*) was her claim of
virginity, her freely offered "yes" to God.

Her entry into my life was not during a time of freedom
or independence on my part. I had no Magnificat to sing. I
was just a washed-up, broken-down drunk, and I was all of
thirty-two years old.

The problem I had was that I was hearing voices — lots and
lots of voices. Some of them came from the social worker and
his rat-pack crowd telling me that it was my drinking that was
making for the stinking thinking. They talked in riddles like
that, words I didn't understand. My boss was telling me that
the rat-pack crowd of recovering alcoholics was the cause of
my inattention at work, and I should just be moderate, not like
those all-or-nothing types. My family thought I had physical
ailments and should see a "physical doctor." My psychiatrist
said the problems were anxiety and sleep-deprivation based,
and easily broken with prescriptions for sleeping pills and anti-
anxiety drugs. My husband was saying nobody died from lack
of sleep, but I sure seemed to be trying hard. He didn't know
what to say. I didn't know what to answer.

So I let myself get swept up into the university infirmary
to buy some time, a little sleep, and a lot of attention while
those voices swirled around outside my door.

It was kind of fun in a perverted way. I fancied the big dramatic hospital scene as long as nothing actually hurt and I could smoke in my room. I was in a reality daytime soap opera, and I had the leading role. It was all fun until my social worker asked me what my long-range plan was when I checked out of the infirmary.

"I'll try a few AA meetings," I said agreeably, to make him happy.

"That's a start," he said.

"There's *more?*" I'd given all I was prepared to give and there was *more?* How about rest and relaxation, which is why I thought I came to the infirmary in the first place?

"There's more," he said, jumping *right* into the opportunity presented. "*Don't* drink. *Do* go to meetings regularly. Do some reading, use the phone, and don't drug."

"I assume you mean recreational drugs. That's not a problem. I'm straight."

"I mean *any* drugs. Don't go home with a full prescription of Xanex."

"That's between me and my doctor. You're not a doctor."

"I'll match my success rate against theirs any day. You won't make it your way or their way. If you fall back on Xanex or whatever you talk the doctors into writing you next, you won't make it. It's the *next* worse thing you could do after drinking. If you're right-handed and you have a choice of which hand to cut off, you'll pick your left hand, but it isn't much of a choice. Regard taking Xanex as chopping off your left hand."

"There goes my last escape," I moaned, finally struck with how awful *all* the world had suddenly become.

"It's not an escape to me," he said flatly. "It's a shovel. Have a good weekend. See you around — maybe."

Now I lay me down to sleep . . . but who the hell can sleep? How would I manage? Would my whole life have to change? Would I have to go to those meetings all the time? Is this like a disease? If you fight very hard for the rest of your life, do you get nothing better than this one-day-at-a-time happy talk remission? I had a boss my age die of leukemia. *Remission* was his word, and it was agony to get there. If he had a choice, would he have taken the agony to get to remission instead of dying? Is that the choice between the left hand or the right hand?

I pray the Lord my soul to keep . . . When I left the infirmary the next morning, I asked my favorite nurse — a woman, like me, from Rhode Island — to *not* give me back the prescriptions that were waiting for the trip home. I didn't know her name, but she had eyes so full of caring that not an ounce of condemnation could slip in. I wanted to remember her eyes for the rest of my life.

"You'll do it," she reassured me as she put the prescriptions back into a folder. "They have these groups now that they didn't have before. And Rhode Islanders are tough."

I wanted to hug her for giving me a piece of dignity, and for putting herself with me in the same class she called "tough Rhode Islanders." I was anything but at that moment. I was broken shards of glass on the bathroom floor, like the poem I'd written on the way to the infirmary:

INFINITY

> You could see yourself forever
> at any given angle.
> You knew all the angles, didn't you,
> and spent hours
> polishing the faces

of one-dimensional mirrors
now shattered in your mind.
What will you look like
when you are free of reflection?

What indeed? A year earlier, my social worker told me the horror story of a secretary at the university who, one day, up and left her desk and killed herself, leaving behind a poem in her typewriter about breaking all the mirrors. He was pretty impressed by the imagery, and all I could think was oh, yuck, how hokey, and Ron, baby, it's been *done!*

I wasn't snickering when Ron, the social worker, left me alone in the dark night of an infirmary with no escape from my demons, and only a shovel to bury myself. I wrote my own hokey little broken-glass poem and didn't care if it was hokey or not.

Before I checked out of the infirmary, I went into the bathroom to look into a real mirror, to assure myself I was still myself. I looked empty and dead like those pathetic old ladies alone in the back of the church. Like them, I began to mumble over and over, *Hail Mary, full of grace, blessed art thou among women.* I didn't know there was more to the prayer, so I said that much over and over.

I almost meant it. I wanted Mary to care and intercede for me. But I didn't quite believe she would or know what it was I was asking for. I was too tired to play games any more. In the shattered mirror, free of reflection, it was Mary who came forward to meet me.

The AA types said I needed a Higher Power. I had problems with Christianity — we had parted company for over a decade. But I wasn't going to ask for help from some formless, vague, bigger-than-me-up-in-the-sky concept either. I needed someone with a name, someone who lived and walked the earth, someone I could talk to, someone who was a woman.

I remembered the Rhode Island nurse and her eyes. I imagined those as Mary's eyes, and how she would have looked at me if we had stood together in the infirmary.

Maybe we did.

I could pray to her. I could let myself do that. Not being brought up Catholic, at least I didn't have any baggage about Mary.

She worked as hard as I did in the weeks that followed — maybe harder. She was as close as my breath, and I was hyperventilating a lot in the early days of sobriety. I needed an AA sponsor. I didn't know how to get one. *Hail Mary, I need a sponsor, and I need one now, help me find one.* Two hours of downtime at the office before my ride home: Do I go to the Student Center for a bagel or to the library and borrow books? Do needlepoint or write in my diary? Work on my resume? Pull out the counted cross-stitch that I counted wrong? Maybe do it all if I schedule my time properly? *Help me slow down, Hail Mary. I've been sick a long time. I'm only beginning to know I was sick and that I'm recovering. I not only need but want to slow down . . .*

Hail Mary never faltered. I spent those two hours watching sailboats on the Charles River, delighting in the view. As my social worker would say, "Time is all we have." And I'd almost spent all of it before I was thirty-five.

It's not something you explain in a van driving away from a strange church and a mysterious ceremony attended by unknown persons. What Hail Mary — as I called her in innocence, not knowing of her finer titles — did was what Hail Mary does. She interceded for me, guided me, listened to me — and ultimately led me to her Son. Once I got there, she moved back a little, into the background of my new life, which included regular churchgoing. I spent four years going to AA meetings. When I knew I could no longer walk that path, I flew back to Boston to sit with Ron one last time.

"Will I get drunk if I don't go to meetings?" I asked point-blank.

"Not necessarily," he answered. "Just don't get isolated."

"I won't. I'm going to become Catholic."

"Wow, you *really* hate those meetings, don't you!"

When I was in sixth grade, I went to confirmation class because that's what you did after fifth grade Sunday school and before you got to stay for the whole church service with the adults. On the appointed Sunday afternoon, I put on the white satiny dress my mother made me, stuck the veil attached to a headband into my hair, and went to church for the second time that day. The bishop was waiting for us.

Our minister said to him, "Reverend Father in God, I present unto you these persons to receive the Laying on of Hands."

The bishop was elderly, kindly, and had a thick British accent. He said a long prayer. We said, "I do," because our confirmation teacher told us to. We said it again when the bishop asked if we would follow Jesus. Then we went up one by one to have the bishop lay hands on our heads. Two of the boys in the class fainted from nerves, heat, or unaccustomed shirt-and-tie combinations. We ate cookies and had our pictures taken as a class with the bishop. We would never have to do this again — or go to Sunday school again either.

But some of us came back, if by a circuitous route, and this time our confirmation became our Magnificat. A Catholic bishop writes, "What Mary says is, although I do not always understand the unfolding of God's plan and God's providential order, nonetheless, if God calls, I accept. If God challenges, I respond."[6]

Nearly a decade after Hail Mary came storming into my life — there was no time for niceties or daintiness; there was *work* to be done! — I returned the favor by choosing freely to re-enter her Son's church, *my* turn to accept God's offer of grace. I said my "yes" at the Easter Vigil, a monstrously long service. Twenty of us were set to go and nineteen showed up, with only the very pregnant one from rehearsal not making it to showtime (not ours, anyway). I was next to last to get the oils dabbed on my forehead, together with the request to fill me with the Holy Spirit.

I was only required to make two responses. The "amen" was beyond me, apparently, and the assisting priest had to fill in. But I managed the second response (*"and also with you"*) complete with eye contact to the pastor.

When I turned to face the congregation, my sponsor told me later, "You were *radiant,* like a bride." I could see him and also a friend who came to bear witness to the moment, and also Felix, and *all* of them were crying. I didn't want to cry at all. My sponsor was right: I felt radiant. *I had done it.*

And surely, I had not done it alone.

The intensity of the relationship with Hail Mary — and my total, unwavering dependence on her — has moderated since I entered the Catholic Church. There are bills to be paid, there is the ordinary dailiness of my work to be done. The sensation of being inside a washing machine during its spin cycle — the way early sobriety felt — is an old memory now.

Sometimes I miss that intensity, if not the life circumstance that led me to Hail Mary. But she remains, willingly, a tool in my trade of Catholicism. On those odd Saturday nights at the local Benedictine abbey, I can chant along with the monks, a valentine offered in the perfect harmony of love.

THREE

The Eucharist

THERE ARE ALL KINDS of tools to meet all kinds of needs. When it comes to the tools I use to stay Catholic, the Eucharist is the most important in my collection. Perhaps it is more like the workbench upon which all the other tools rest. Without this Eucharist, I am nothing. Without it, I am certainly not Catholic.

Unlike some of the other tools, this one is not about personal prayer style or what flavor jimmies I want sprinkled on my ice-cream cone. I share this tool with every other practicing Catholic. It is a tool of remembrance, an offering of grace made by Christ himself, the carpenter's apprentice.

I was on the lector schedule for the 5:30 p.m. Saturday Vigil Mass the third week of Easter. In a church that counts its membership in the thousands, and every Mass has a hunt-for-a-seat contest by the opening hymn, I am heartened by the liveliness of the faith. But I am not so happy by the lack of quietness and preparedness that precedes the celebration of the Eucharist. Those fifteen minutes before Mass begins reach the noise level of happy hour, and sometimes Max, the cantor, can barely be heard over the loudspeaker system as he tries to announce the opening hymn.

I compensate by getting to the church thirty minutes before Mass begins. That gives me fifteen minutes to sit in the cool, darkened, quiet church I love so much, to meditate in the light of the sun reflecting off the Pacific Ocean just a few miles below us. I listen to the muted sounds of rosary beads clicking together by another solitary early worshipper far from me, hear the occasional sob from someone else deep in petition on her knees, and the sigh of the man lost in prayer before the San Damiano Crucifix in the furthest corner of the church. It is a time to recollect myself after a rough-and-tumble week of day duty as a lobbyist and nights as wife, daughter, artist, and gym rat. It's my time alone with God. And on those evenings when I'm the lector, it's my time to move from practicing the readings to praying them before I get up and proclaim them to the congregation.

Coming to church early also has its less noble benefits. I get the best parking space in our church's meager lot, and I get to stake out *my* chosen spot to sit in the church– front left, second row, end seat.

Not *this* night, no sirree, not this thirty minutes before what I thought was only the Third Sunday of Easter. I knew something was up when I arrived in the parking lot, and not only was *my* parking spot, but a whole lot of *other* people's spots were occupied at the not-yet-godly hour of 5:00 p.m. The entry to the church was also occupied by adults and children milling around the bride's room, which was now labeled "Photographer" and hosted a woman at a card table clearly selling something.

Every anti-people instinct in me — and, unfortunately, I possess a lot of those instincts — told me to turn on my heel and bail out while there was still time. I've done it before when I've seen the Knights of Columbus brandishing swords outside the church. But this Third Sunday of Easter was also my turn to read as lector, so I shrugged off the early-crowd factor and entered the church proper.

The place was swarming with little girls, *lousy* with little starter brides running around in white dresses and veils. They, at least, looked like they were having fun. Uncharacteristically, it was the little boys who stayed put in their long pants, long ties, and long faces. This is southern California in May. Nobody their age dresses like that by choice, even for church, during short-pant season. Obviously, coercion was involved, at least for the boys.

The source of coercion was evident all about: the parents with video cameras, with digital equipment, with old-fashioned flash photography, and with quickie disposable cameras. They ran around posing the little brides and long-faced grooms in the various religious hot-spot Kodak moments found all over the church. No statue, no cross, no candle was safe from the marauding band of photographer-parents. There was no hush for the clack of rosary beads and no room on the kneeler at the San Damiano Crucifix for the sighs of the penitent. And, worst of insults, my seat was taken up by some Kodak parent!

"What in the *world* is going on?" I hissed at Father Don as he emerged from the confessional to set up at the altar and turn up the lights.

"*Surely* you can figure it out?" he asked, barely breaking stride. "First Communion today."

So this is what it looks like. I knew the words and I've seen those photographs from black-and-white days, of angelic girls looking heavenward and prayerful with rosary beads entwined around their clasped baby hands. They were photos from a long-ago childhood, and not *my* childhood at all.

"Episcopal kids don't do First Communion," I said to Father Don. "We got confirmed in sixth grade and Communion was part of the ceremony."

"Wouldn't fly with Catholics," he said. "We tried moving First Communion to fourth or fifth grade, but the parents complained. They felt it was too important to let their children wait so long." As he hurried off to put on his vestments, he added over his shoulder, "By the way, you won't be reading tonight. The children do it."

Phooey. Why am I here for this Madhouse Mass at all then, and in particular, *why* am I here thirty minutes early? I've bailed at less, but this time somebody forgot to call off the lector.

As soon as the Kodak parent took off to find another shot for her little angel, I charged over to take *my* seat for what was obviously going to be a very long Vigil Mass. "I've never experienced First Communion," I said to fellow lectors who came and sat behind me when they found out all the adult lector readings were off. "I'm a convert."

"But you still made a *first* Communion," he said. "We all did."

"Yeah, but I didn't get a new dress or a picture out of it."

So when was my First Communion? When did it count? The first Communion after being received into the Catholic Church during the longest Easter Vigil Mass I had ever experienced, too excited and prideful (*I did it!*) to know anything beyond my four guests in the family row? The Communion I took the day I first walked into a Catholic church to see what it was all about, too innocent to read the back of the missalette for exclusionary clauses? Was it the first time I approached the altar in these mega-churches with their casts of thousands, and the priest said, "Body of Christ, Carol," as if I had somehow been called by name for such an honor?

They were all First Communions, maybe not in the eyes of the church, but for me.

When it comes to the centrality of the Eucharist, I've been both sides of center, which gives me a different perspective. When she was mistakenly referred to as a convert to Catholicism, the *very* Catholic writer Flannery O'Connor once huffed, "I think there is usually a difference in the way converts write and the way the born variety write. With the born variety, the point of view is more naturally integrated into the personality, or such is my theory."[1] I chose Catholicism, and brought the baggage of other ways with me, not integrated at all, but with the sense of wonder and choice of the Eucharist's meaning.

The Episcopal Church I grew up in made many changes to its worship about the time Catholicism was shedding many of *its* old ways. In its old ways, the "low" Episcopal church in my neighborhood leaned toward plainer, Protestant-style coloration versus the "high" churches of the city with their incense and fancy ways. Every week our church services came from the Book of Common Prayer's morning prayer service with readings, Psalter, hymns, prayers, and sermon (or Sunday school until you got confirmed). When the Camp Fire Girls went to church together once a year, all of us, except the Catholic girls (who weren't allowed to go to a non-Catholic church) went to the Congregational church where our Camp Fire Girl meetings met. The only difference I could see between them and my regular service as an Episcopalian was that I didn't know as many of their hymns as I did mine.

But once a month — and how we all dreaded it, even some of the adults — we had the Holy Communion service. In my home, it was simply called, "the long service." It seemed to have *all* the parts of morning prayer — readings, Psalter, hymns, prayers, *and* sermon — *plus* all the extra prayers of the Holy Communion service, *and* everybody going up to the rail for Communion as well. *Would this thing never end?*

When my family went camping during summer weekends, we attended a church in a town too small to support both a Methodist and Episcopal Church. One week, the plain little white wooden church was Methodist, the next week Episcopal. My sister and I were a fit of giggles at the unexpectedness of the Methodist Holy Communion. Grape juice was poured into little shot glasses for you to take from a tray, individually consumed, and neatly returned, along with a side of cubed white bread (no crusts) for you to chew.

This was the stuff of symbol, the elements of ordinary food. We thought it looked pretty funny in church.

On the other hand, my mother allowed us to partake on Methodist communion days. Not yet confirmed, we were not allowed to partake of the Episcopal elements. I assumed the difference was between wine and grape juice, but she knew it was the difference in consecration.

The Eucharist is that consecration of ordinary elements, from foodstuffs to the most sacred food and drink, and even more — "a joyful banquet" as one writer expresses it, "a living memorial, the representation of the very death and resurrection of the Lord for our time and place."[2]

There is a fine little Congregational church on the island of Kauai in the small town of Hanalei. During one trip to the island, we read of how the choir there sings in the old Hawaiian ways you will never hear in the upscale mega-resort area. So Felix and I hauled down the one-lane road from Princeville to experience the 9:00 a.m. service. Because Felix is not a churchgoer, I forgot that as a small boy he went through the motions of Catholic churchgoing. "I was even an altar boy," he confessed once. "It didn't take."

When we got to the church, it was as wonderfully local as anything we'd encountered in our Hawaiian vacations. The pastor was retired from Oceanside, California — just ten miles from where we lived, and was called to serve as interim minister while the church searched for its new permanent one. The interim was joyous, amazed at God's Providence in landing him and his wife in Kauai for a year, kindly with his temporary flock. His wife's strudel was freshly baked in the rectory oven and waiting for us all to take a taste after the service. The choir was all Hawaiian, and Sunday hymns never sounded as sweet as when accompanied by guitar, two ukuleles, and an ipu.

The service lasted forever, or so it seemed to Felix. A half hour into the sermon, with no "in conclusion" anywhere on the horizon, he leaned over and whispered, "Is this all they're going to do? Sing and talk?" I had also not realized that his entire childhood churchgoing experience was limited to Catholic Mass — and, furthermore, in the old Latin-language days with the priest's back to the congregation. He'd never been to a Protestant service where, indeed, this singing and preaching, along with praying, is "all they do." He was waiting for the Eucharistic moment without necessarily knowing it as such.

The Eucharist — "communion" is the word for its distribution — is my essential Catholic tool. I can get it nowhere else, and to be denied it would send me into spiritual exile. I saw the edge of exile at, of all places, a small Mass at a religious retreat center in Arizona where I was finishing up a conference. Holy Eucharist was offered every morning if we cared to join the religious community in residence. But

I did not care to join them at 7:00 a.m., and the later Mass would interfere with conference sessions. The time change for me, coming from California, coupled with the absurd idea of such early rising on a weekend, combining with the desire to be first in the breakfast line, gave me reasons enough to skip the weekday option for Holy Eucharist without guilt. But Sunday attendance was a different matter, although they still celebrated Mass too early for me.

"You can go to their other Mass across the street," someone told me. "It's a private retreat center, but you're allowed to join them for Mass in their chapel. It's an hour later than ours."

That was doable, especially for a Sunday. The psalm I was meditating on that week encouraged me to brave the unknown chapel and its private enclave of guests. *I keep the Lord ever in my sight,* sings a song of David, *since he is at my right hand, I shall stand firm.*[3]

I liked that verse, and whispered it with each step as I walked away from my familiar little conference gathering, name badge firmly in place, to find this other place, other chapel. In this psalm, it isn't love that God returns to us. It is the strength of God's presence that He gives. Presence matters, yes it does.

Had it not been for the presence of a writer from New York, I would have given up the idea of Mass at all that morning. When I found the chapel, the door was closed. When I opened it, ten sets of eyes opened and turned to look at me. There was meditation music droning softly in the background, and I had interrupted something and ten someones.

There was a big bear of a man coming toward the chapel as I was beating a hasty retreat from it.

"How's the conference going?" he asked.

"The confer...?" I forgot I had my name badge on, like a neon sign that flashed, NOT ONE OF US..."It's good, very good. What's going on inside? I thought there was Mass."

"Oh there is. Most of the people staying here practice centering prayer for an hour first. That would put me to sleep, so I just come for Mass. You can go in."

"After you," I said, not from graciousness, but from the desire to avoid those ten sets of eyes on me again.

"I'm David," he said before we entered. "I'm a writer, here from New York."

"I'm Carol," I said, shaking his hand. "From San Diego." Then I slipped inside the chapel behind his bigness and let him take the hit of those staring eyes. Presence matters a *lot*.

It was a long, drawn-out service, but that made sense, since it was the only experience of community this group would know all day before returning to their hermitages and silences. When it came time for the Eucharist, there was an elaborate shuffling and snaking about. I thought I would be first up, since I took the only empty seat when I entered, and it was closest to the altar. In fact, in our serpentine way, I ended up at the end of the line.

As we shuffled forward, I realized that for all his physical bulk, David, the writer from New York, was a physical wreck. His hands and arms twitched without stopping, and he shuffled along toward the altar on buckling, shaky legs. The strength I borrowed to enter the chapel was not as rock-like as I had presumed.

We reached the altar. The Eucharistic minister placed the last consecrated Host into David's twitching hands and then turned away with her empty bowl and left the altar. I saw what happened from behind David's back, and I couldn't believe it: *they had consecrated exactly enough to take care of their registered* guests. The stranger in their midst, with her "Hello! I'm Carol" badge on her tee shirt, was hardly being welcomed as Christ.

Here I stood at the altar, with my begging hands lifted for Christ, and my uplifted hands were going to be ignored and left empty. I saw what had happened, and I knew why it had happened, but I couldn't believe it was happening. If it *was* really happening, and I was going to be left at the altar with my begging hands empty and those ten pairs of eyes politely lowered from my shame — well, I knew I would leave the altar. I would walk past my seat that was so close that I thought I'd be first, and I would continue out the door, past the eyes, and never return. Because I knew that if I was left empty, begging for Christ, there was nothing in this church for me either, that it was as empty as my hands.

David, the writer from New York, turned away from the fleeing Eucharistic minister and her empty bowl, literally turned his back on the altar made by human hands, and became, himself, the altar made by God. He broke his Host with his trembling, twitching hands, held one half of it up, and looked at me. "The body of Christ, Carol."

"Amen."

God was ever in my sight, at my right hand. I could stand firm again in the shadow of this shaking giant. I had tasted near-exile, and was grateful beyond belief to be returned.

I was a college student when the real significance of the Eucharist came to my attention for the first time. I joke now that because I wasn't Catholic in those days my parents couldn't send me to a convent to break my wildness. They sure outdid themselves in parental imagination, though, sending me instead to an obsessively conservative, square-cornered, Bible-thumping Southern Baptist college — in New England, no less.

"They had a good music school," my mother still says, defending this screwball choice of college. She even still sends them money during the annual alumni-parent drive, against my squeals of protest.

"Ma, they were *nutcases*. You guys sent me to a nutcase college just because I was a little wild." The nutcases thought that women wearing pants to college — and New England winters could get pretty cold — was immoral, as well as drinking, smoking, dancing, playing cards, or being an Episcopalian. Episcopalians were practically *papist,* not that these guys knew what "papists" were really like, since Catholics, sensibly, stayed far away from this nutcase place.

Not only was chapel compulsory, but so was an academic-minor concentration in biblical theology. It didn't matter if you majored in music, math, or modern languages; you minored in biblical theology.

"Ma! I went to college to major in music! What were you thinking?"

"I was thinking I never heard you swear before you went to college, and once you got to that nice Christian college, I never heard you *stop* swearing. . . . "

"They were *nutcases*, Ma. Screaming, loony tunes *nutcases!*"

One professor, who was marvelously sane and learned, had my respect if not my attention or study devotion. An ordained Baptist minister as well as New Testament and biblical theology professor, Dr. Buehlman was kindly and thoughtful, and gave our questions and concerns more consideration than they probably merited. And because of his kindness, he was one of the few I listened to in the years when I didn't listen to very much.

In his New Testament History, Religion, and Culture class — mandatory for second-semester freshmen — he gamely tackled the words of the Last Supper ("*take, eat . . . this is my Body . . . this is my Blood . . .*"). These commands appear in the three Synoptic Gospels of Matthew, Mark, and Luke, and have echoes in John's discourse on the bread of life. (*For my flesh is true food and my blood is true drink. . . .*[4])

Dr. Buehlman grimly compared Gospel versions out loud, sighed, and said, "This is where we part company with the Roman Catholic Church. This is the place where Catholics say that it is what Jesus says it is, and where we literal-minded Baptists say, well, not so fast there. . . ."

A few students squirmed with his visible discomfort. The rest of us waited to see how he'd get out of *this* one. But he sighed, and went on with his lecture about how such language even in those times, disturbed, disgusted, and frightened people, and how some of the followers left Jesus over the meaning of those words.

I made an appointment to meet Dr. Buehlman during office hours — the only such appointment I ever scheduled with anybody over the four years I was an undergraduate.

"So what am I supposed to *do*?" I demanded.

"About what?" He glanced at his grade book and no doubt wondered how much extra credit could exist to bring up my dismal grades.

"About the Last Supper. I think Jesus meant what he said."

Dr. Buehlman looked straight at me and saw me for the first time all semester. "I think so too," he said. "I lack the imagination to think the words he said were anything but the literal truth he needed to tell us. It's just that I also lack the imagination to follow through on the implications of what those words might mean."

"So if I don't believe everything a church says, only some of it, do I go out and start a new church?"

"Oh heavens, no!" he said quickly, and then laughed. "We Baptists have been doing that pretty well. Don't follow our footsteps."

"Well, then, whose footsteps do I follow?"

He stopped laughing and sighed the difficult sigh of a thinker in a place that desired unambiguous answers. "Follow the one you believe. The rest will fall in place or fall away and won't matter anyway."

It took me nearly twenty years before I followed the one I believed, and answered "amen," and received his Body and Blood. Once in, I couldn't imagine how I would ever leave. I don't mean *that* literally. It is very easy for me to see the speck in the church's eye while ignoring the planks in my own.[5] I go through stages where any excuse is a good enough excuse to leave the church that I once wanted so badly to enter.

There are always obstacles, like Dr. Buehlman's lack of imagination, as he called it, to the implications of the Eucharist. Some are obstacles of my own making; others are carefully placed there by the church because it is not good enough for the church that I believe, but that I believe correctly. Imagination itself can be a hindrance that the church itself tries to remove. "It is not as though Jesus took on a miniature body to be present in the Eucharist or as though he were present in a natural but hidden way beneath a layer of bread and wine," writes Bishop Wuerl.[6] "It is a supernatural mystery that the person who becomes fully present at Mass is the same Risen Savior who is seated at the right hand of the Father."

Well, okay, if that's helpful to you guys, but I need images. *What does it look like?*

Felix was on one of his adventures to China — Shanghai this time — when he slipped into a Buddhist temple teeming with the devout. One photograph he took to show me was less than stunning to view: a young woman with a backpack, hands pressed together, head bowed, in front of a large iron bell suspended a few feet above the ground.

"What's she doing?" I asked, mostly to be polite, because Felix seemed so thrilled at the photo. "Is she praying to a bell?"

"That's exactly what I thought," Felix said excitedly, "and I couldn't imagine why she would do that, so I got as close as I could, and I zoomed in with the camera, and now here it is."

He showed me his next photo. Up close and zoomed in, there was a statue of Buddha under the bell, along with flowers, fruits, and other offerings. It was a picture of the inside of worship, the hidden life, hidden inside the bell.

What a wonderful thing to have seen, I thought, the sacred within the ordinary that proclaims it, Buddha in a bell! If Felix were taking photos during Mass, could he get close enough, zoom in enough, to see Christ in the Eucharist? No. But that only makes our experience even more wonderful to behold, away from a literal camera-kind of knowing, to knowing with the eyes of faith alone. There is a lifetime of gratitude available to me in being saved by Christ, and in being called by Christ. There is a lifetime of privileges in answering that call. The Eucharist reminds me. I am fortunate that others have pointed out the Buddha under the bell.

"The Eucharist is at the center of the church's life," continues Bishop Wuerl in a series of essays written as reflections on the *Catechism of the Catholic Church*. "In the celebration of this mystery of faith, Christ himself is present to his people."[7]

And, so far at least, I find that to be an invitation to a celebration that I cannot possibly walk away from and say, "No thanks; better offer elsewhere." Because, so far at least, there *is* no better offer elsewhere. And I doubt there will be a better offer anytime soon, at least while I'm on this end of the journey to the New Jerusalem.

If that's what we find when we receive the Eucharist, what is it Christ sees when we receive him?

A Eucharistic minister suggests it well when he talks about his ministry, of "giving Christ to those holier than me, who walk up with such reverence, simplicity, seriousness, and childlike vulnerability that my eyes sometimes film with tears. . . . " He goes on to say, "For I have just an inkling of what Jesus felt when he looked on his friends in mercy and aching love, and I have a sense of why, just before he died, he established this gracious sacrament of himself."[8]

When I am preparing for Mass as a lector, I frequently hear the Eucharistic ministers speak in unusually hushed tones about the great honor of their ministry. This night, though, they were carefully counting ministers and battle stations, and who did what and when, for it was First Communion, officially, with the new dresses and photos, and the old-timers wanted it done right for the young ones.

The children were well-rehearsed. They read the lessons and the intercessions and brought the gifts up to the altar with heartbreaking care and attention, and finally were ready to receive their First Communion.

This is how they came to meet Christ in the Eucharist for the first time: prideful, sweet, fidgety, terrified, indifferent, and reverent.

They approached Christ in the Eucharist with their parents. Some parents joined in the Eucharist. Others, divided by faith, came forward with crossed arms the way their children had done until this night. Some of the children came forward alone. They seemed to approach with the most defiance, as if challenging the right to be there at all.

One little boy's Communion experience revolved not around whom he was to receive, but who would receive it with him — his badly emaciated, wheelchair-bound father. When it was his turn to come forward, the little boy waited until his father was in position to wheel up to the altar before they faced Christ in the Eucharist. Where most of the girls had their attention on the Host, and most of the boys had their attention on the floor, this one little boy's entire attention and being was focused on his father.

After Communion, the children were grouped together in front of the altar to sing and sign-language a simple song. Of the 1,800 people in that congregation, that little boy sang and signed to the one emaciated, terribly wasted young man, his father — and surely it was the love of God who shone back from his father's unwavering eyes.

You never know what you'll get at Mass when you show up. I *came* to do the second reading for the Third Sunday after Easter. Instead, I tasted Christ, got close enough to see the Buddha under the bell, and witnessed a father's love.

FOUR

Novenas

W HEN FAMILIES ARE ARTIFICIALLY BLENDED in the ways marriage and remarriage can do, the result is like a piece of collage art: elements from many lives and histories are pulled out of their original context and pasted together to form an entirely new — and frequently chaotic — work of art.

Such families are living collages of old tastes, habits, and family lore, suddenly lifted out and repositioned into a new context. When we blended a family out of Felix, his two children, and me, I was outnumbered three-to-one. What that meant: I *never* got the family joke, or understood their putting mustard in the refrigerator (since *my* people knew it belonged in the pantry), or accepted the dogs-are-better-pets-than-cats theory.

It was the family jokes referencing family lore and wisdom resulting from one of those experiences you had to be there to appreciate, now reduced to a punch line over time that could really drive me batty. My first winter in the Bonomo household in Stow, Massachusetts was a classic winter wonderland of white snow, bleak bare trees, and ice-covered bird feeders out in the country, outside of Boston where I worked.

Unfortunately, the winter wonderland in that area began a week after the leaves fell from the trees. It lasted long after Easter, no matter *how* late Easter came. But I didn't know any of that the first year, only how beautiful it all looked, how charming to live in a classic Colonial house, in apple country, with a bird feeder outside the kitchen windows.

The bird feeder particularly caught my fancy, since I'd moved there from downtown Boston, and nobody had bird feeders when the only birds we ever saw were pigeons.

"Absolutely not," Felix said when I mentioned getting bird feed for the feeder. "Do you see how far that feeder is from the house or the back porch? Do you know how impossible it will be to get feed in the feeder after the fifth or sixth snowstorm when the backyard has snow up to the bottom of the kitchen windows for a month or more?"

That didn't seem to be a good reason against putting out some bird feed now, in glorious early fall, so we could enjoy the birds eating their breakfasts while we ate ours. "We don't have to do it forever —," I began.

It was as if I had suddenly crossed over an invisible line — invisible only to me. Felix and his children suddenly chanted in perfect unison, *"Once you start ... "*

"Once you start *what?* Feeding the birds? Then what?"

"Once you start, you can't stop," the two kids chanted. Felix snickered.

It was their family teaching moment, saying "hello" to the newest family member. Especially out in the country, and certainly during the long, frequently harsh winters, those birds who stuck it out with us, and those who had come from as far as Canada to winter here in Massachusetts, worked hard on their food supply lines when the ground was covered and the trees were bare. Once they learned of a regular food source — God alone knew *how* they learned of it — they would quickly come to depend on it.

"You don't want the birds to *die,* do you?" my stepdaughter asked, all big, horrified eyes.

"No. I just want to know why you have a bird feeder in the middle of a snowfield with no plans to feed birds. It's not like one stupid bird feeder is going to keep all the birds in the neighborhood *alive.* ... "

"But once you *start* ... " she began again.

"I know. I know!" My blended family knew an important lesson about the spiritual virtues of perseverance in that little phrase and the facts of nature it represented.

To learn and appreciate the spiritual tool of perseverance — and how it keeps my Catholic faith alive especially in tough times or dry spells or cranky Catholic days — I discovered the lovely staying power of novenas.

Novena means *nine,* and at its simplest means nine days of devotion or prayer. One writer describes novenas as "an occasion of prayer and intercession."[1] But that is to take it literally, stripped of the unique qualities of language and emotion that set novenas apart from other devotional practices, and make "doing a novena" quite different from anything else I'm "doing."

Novenas originated in the Middle Ages to prepare the faithful for Christmas. It's possible that the "O antiphons" sung by my Benedictine monks (among others) beginning on December 17 and ending on December 24 may be the historical remnants of old liturgical practices resembling a nine-day prayer. The Christmas novenas recalled to mind Mary's nine months of pregnancy. Other novenas developed in the Middle Ages. For instance, one novena of that time prays for the gifts of the Holy Spirit and recalls the nine days the apostles and Mary waited after the ascension of Jesus for the coming of the Spirit, or Pentecost. My friend Sister Edna loves to call this one "the first novena" because it signifies the time of waiting and praying and undoubtedly a great bit of intense emotion, as these people who so loved Jesus waited in hope for a promise to be fulfilled. While it may not be a first novena in literal terms, it is one of the oldest official novenas and is still the only one officially prescribed by the church.[2]

Novenas were nearly always prayers of intercession — to favorite angels, to the Blessed Mother, and, in the case of Sister Edna's first novena, to God in the Holy Spirit — usually prompted by urgent need, frequently for healings. By the seventeenth century, novenas also honored particular saints, especially Mary in all her titles, and prepared the faithful for major feasts. In the nineteenth century, the church began issuing indulgences for some novenas. Dianne Bergant, in an article on novenas for *America* magazine, notes that the Raccolta, or official book of indulgences, lists more than thirty indulgenced novenas.[3]

There are at least eleven official novenas to Mary, and she is the most popular for relief from guilt, family discord, and souls in distress. Angels, such as Raphael, Michael, Gabriel, and guardian angels, are evoked for petitions that affect the way our lives are going or need to go. The saints are usually of interest for material or health problems, and many carry specialties like cancer (St. Peregrine), finding a job (St. Joseph), or arthritis and old age (St. Alphonsus).

But any saint or angel can be appealed to — it seems to be part of the heavenly host's job description. Given the human needs and desperation that can drive many novenas, I suspect that whether or not they are indulgenced matters less to ordinary folks than that they work. Based on word-of-mouth effectiveness, St. Anthony of Padua and St. Jude are top of the charts in popularity, and, presumably, effectiveness.

Of all the kinds of prayers in our toolboxes, novenas are marked by their language, art, and effect upon the pray-er with their intensity. The rosary is contemplative, as are the stations of the cross. The Mass is celebration and memorial all in one. The Divine Office brings the whole church together in its prayer. Novenas, too, have become more celebratory in nature, such as commemorating a feast or preparing for a particular saint's day. One writer notes that such celebratory novenas provide her with the time "to reflect on the significance of these issues for my own life." She goes on to say, "Novenas have become times of preparation for some change that I must make in my life, rather than times of 'storming heaven' for a favor."[4]

As a Benedictine oblate, I appreciate some of the celebratory novenas too. I try to pray the novena to St. Benedict before the Feast of his passing (March 21, and nearly always in Lent) and the Solemnity of St. Benedict and All Benedictine Saints (July 11, when I also have the opportunity to remember my Benedictine patroness, Blessed Joanna Mary). It is not a petitionary novena, but one that celebrates Benedict as saint, monk, father, lawgiver, miracle worker, prophet, teacher, apostle, and man of God. It is a beautiful opportunity to live nine days in the spirit of my spiritual guide.

Some novenas combine preparation and petition, such as the novena to St. Joseph, which is said to be particularly effective as a petition if done for the seven Sundays prior to his feast day — those seven Sundays representing his seven sorrows and seven joys.[5] But it's still supposed to be prayed nine days in a row, so I, for one, don't understand how to make the *math* work.

But the most loved and prayed novenas are painfully personal and petitionary. Perhaps the naked honesty of appealing for help in desperate circumstances is what appeals to me. This is not the tool of clear reason or the perfection that prayers of praise possess. This is the tool of an obsessive worry (and worrier) crying out to God and favorite saints for assistance. To me, this is the long-drawn-out prayer of the end-of-the-line nothing-to-loser. Its beauty comes from the brokenness of the pray-er. God seems able to penetrate my life more when I am broken than when I am whole and "full of myself," as the expression accurately goes.

It is not a highly intellectual exercise, which is probably why novenas are frequently tainted in some minds as being close to superstition: *say this prayer nine times a day for nine days and no request will be refused* — well, that can approach a magic formula and cookbook prayer recipe if I just look at the formula. But instead of looking at the prayer, look at the pray-er: generally in a situation of great need, such that all intellectual fences are down anyway. We are not praying *about* pain; we *are* pain.

Novenas were not part of my RCIA experience, and if I knew anything on the subject, it was those little ads placed in the personal section of the newspaper, usually to St. Jude, saying, "Thank you, St. Jude, for prayers answered," and looking more like a chain letter than anything of serious religious content.

And then, early in conversion, I hit naked neediness. I was on my first retreat, with women from my church, and it could have been a wonderful experience to spend the weekend with such thoughtful, prayerful people and stay at a wonderful old Franciscan mission. But I was consumed with the battle drawn up from my divorce from cigarettes. Smoking wanted me back, even though we had been separated for six months. Still, smoking would forgive me everything if only I would return. I cried all the time and scared the other women on the retreat. They would ask me how I was doing and then offer to pray for me when I started crying again.

What was I supposed to say? *No?* Putting down my last drink seven years earlier had given me cause for tears and some raw sewage of feelings rushing out once their swimming hole was gone. Smoking may be a killer, but *not* smoking was doing a pretty good number on me at that point.

With all those women praying for me, I wondered if there weren't also prayers I could say to relieve me of my misery. I had been a Catholic for less than a year, a lost soul in the wilderness for the fifteen years before that. Where to look for answers?

I looked up demons in the Bible to see what people did then to remove them that I was not doing. There were fewer miracles involving demons than I remembered from my Bible studies in college (and fewer than I wanted to see at that time). In the Old Testament, the demons were responsible for mental problems, terrors, temptations, and perversions. By the end of Jesus' ministry, the persona of Satan or the Devil comes more into focus. I had the Old Testament kind, I decided, and read its diagnosis: *The spirit of the Lord had departed from Saul, and he was tormented by an evil spirit....* [6]

Saul's servants offered to find a musician to play and make him feel better. David was who they found, and every time Saul was tormented by his demons, David would take the harp and play. Saul would be relieved and feel better, for the evil spirit would leave him.

Now *that* was the music I needed to find ...

Answers have funny shapes to them when the questions themselves are so formless. While power walking the half-mile, life-sized stations of the cross — I was hardly in the meditative stroll mode of the fellow retreatants that I buzzed by — the stations reminded me of language the Catholic Church spoke when I was a kid and thought it was the most beautiful, exotic church in the world. It used to speak in Latin, in stations, rosaries, blessed mothers, and little flowers, all languages seemingly dead in the church where I had finally arrived twenty years later. The first prayer I learned that helped me escape the alcohol addiction's demon clutches was the Hail Mary. My Marian language had a heavy accent and serious grammatical errors, but I spoke it from a desperate heart, and I had been saved from alcoholism. I needed her now to stay away from cigarettes.

At the mission's bookstore, I found plastic rosaries available free with any purchase (a sign, I thought!) and a book that spelled out something called a novena rosary. I'd never seen any kind of novenas, so I peeked inside. You pray this novena with the "Lively Hope of having your request granted," it said, but also with the "Perfect Resignation that *some* grace or blessing" would result, even if the request itself was not granted.

I was ready for anything lively, and even Perfect Resignation has a nice sound when you feel like hell on legs, so I took it, plus my free, plastic rosary starter kit. There were bunches of nine-day novenas for bunches of special requests and graces, but I was desperate, so I chose a fifty-four-day novena devotion figuring that it would give me enough time to become demon-free or shoot my brains out if the demon was still around. Originating in 1884 at the Sanctuary of Our Lady of the Rosary of Pompeii, it consisted of a daily recitation of five decades of the rosary for twenty-seven days of petition (three novenas' worth), and twenty-seven days of recitation of five decades in thanksgiving (three more novenas) for a particular favor.

It practically needed its own scheduling calendar and calculator, but it gave me something to do with my hands, other than wringing them or sticking a cigarette between my fingers, and a way of occupying at least a small part of the endless days of struggle.

Nine days later, I felt better than at any time in the six months preceding the retreat. I could almost *feel* the addiction pulling away from me, undoubtedly unable to be heard for all the competition of good words and prayers. Alcoholics Anonymous taught me that addiction is a disease which could be arrested but never cured. I didn't believe it. During that first spiritual retreat, I came to know addictions as demons. As demons, they could be removed. The rosary novena was the tool of surgical removal.

Another nine days, another novena of petition completed. I took mental stock before plunging into the last round of petitioning novena. The demon was definitely leaving. It was a hard thing to describe, but I felt it leaving like a guest inside my body that overstayed its welcome and was finally, reluctantly, pulling out because it had been replaced by a new, more welcome guest who was settling in for a long stay.

Faith is such a funny commodity. Sure, I believe in the good news of the Gospels, and in the efficacy of prayers, and even in the petitions being granted. But when I saw that rosary novena in the bookstore — even without knowing the ins and outs of the devotion, where it had come from or who was tops on the charts of best results — there was a rightness and absolute faith in it that surprised me. *She will not deny me my request,* I thought, and there was no further question in my mind to be answered. Hail Mary had been there when I asked to have the desire for a drink removed and it was granted to me, an unbeliever. Now, seven years later, I was back, this time seeking a cure.

And it *was* working, but that aspect did not surprise me as much as the absolute faith on which I embarked on my first novena. But time and temptation turned the wheels on me again.

Day 48 of 54, I was still at it, but more out of pagan superstition of what would happen if I "broke the spell." If I *needed* a novena, why couldn't I have picked an ordinary old nine-day thing you could say and be done with? Noooooooooo, I went with the rosary one and the super-duper fifty-four-day special at that. I was tired of the whole thing. I wanted it to be over and for it to stop taking over my prayer life.

Besides, it wasn't working anymore. It was when I wanted it to be a success story, but by day 48, it was getting in my way. Smoking was calling me, and my prayers were softer, more reluctant to call back.

I returned to smoking a month or so later, which was about how long I needed to bury my intentions with justifications. I had long ago buried both Lively Hope and Perfect Resignation, and certainly forgot all about Some Grace that should have rewarded my efforts.

Novenas are not much in favor these days with the changes of focus since Vatican III emphasizing public liturgy rather than private devotions. The perception of novenas as "magical," and the conviction that many of the prayers sounded like we were begging God for the salvation already granted through Christ's death and resurrection, assisted their demise from daily Catholicism.

Additionally, many novenas developed around health and healing issues. For those issues, our faith now resides in

medical doctors. When doctors fail, there are herbal treatments, magnetic bracelets, and experimental cures south of
the border. The nakedness of need is transferred to other
kinds of faith. And even when prayers *are* requested — say, to
the grandmother who has a novena for every symptom — it's
sometimes more an effort to cover the bases, not the mark of
faith and neediness.

Finally, the prayers of the novena usually contain a unique,
florid language which can be distancing when you read them
under an ordinary light. For example:

> *By the great love which your immaculate spouse had for
> you, O glorious Saint Lucy, when by an unheard-of miracle
> he rendered you immovable in spite of the attempts of your
> enemies to drag you into a place of shame and sin, I ask you
> to obtain for me the grace never to consent to the temptations
> of the world, the flesh, and the devil, and to fight constantly
> against their assaults by the continuous mortification of all
> my senses.*[7]

In her iconography, St. Lucy stands serenely, eyes heavenward, holding in one hand the palms of martyrdom and the
sword that cut her throat. In her other hand, she holds a plate
that carries her eyes, ripped out during torture and miracu-
lously restored. This is a woman with guts (which at least are
not shown in her portrait), a woman to pray to when a pray-er
is in agony for her mother facing a surgery that may repair or
destroy her vision. But the prayers are barely prayable, and I
risk laughing in disrespect.

The language and artwork of the Middle Ages is probably
too jarring and lurid for our times, even though we hardly
live in lavender and lilies. There are times I stumble through
a novena's prayer language like I am wearing somebody else's

clothes that badly cover my nakedness. As writer Flannery O'Connor commented once in a letter, "You feel you are wearing somebody else's finery, and I can never describe my heart as 'burning' to the Lord (who knows better) without snickering."[8] If they're too dated and not timeless, they will cease to become alive for our needs too.

There's no rule that says you can't use prayers of your own heart, or even the artwork of your own times or hands in praying a novena. I think the perseverance and petition of novenas require a bit more of us, however, than *please, please, help, help* — although I pray that way as well.

Advice to novice novenamakers on how to pray them suggests "familiarizing yourself with the images and stories accompanying the prayers. Any saint or angel who feels familiar and sympathetic to you can be asked to intercede for anything."[9] And then there's the Fortune Cookie Cure Novena for Blown Shoulders.

I *know* how I tore my stupid shoulder. I was being a jock. In my mind, especially when I'm at the gym, I think I am a big jock instead of a twerpy, middle-aged-and-then-some lady. In my mind, in the gym, I am *never* a lady.

The trainer at the gym must have read my mind. "Here, let me show you a better way to do a tricep lateral pulldown," he said. He illustrated the better way. I copied him. I felt the tear almost with the first repetition, but I kept at it. Grunt, grunt, no pain, no gain.

The gain must have been great because I never had more than a day of no pain after that. I tried to build up around the pain. I tried going through it. I convinced myself that the pain was all in my mind. My shoulder got really stubborn and said, *Not in your mind, Stupid; here.*

When I could sleep no more than two hours at a stretch and not at all on one side, and my relatively good sense of humor was turning into vinegar, I finally made an appointment with my primary-care physician.

"How long has this been a problem?" he asked as he poked and muttered and did doctorly things.

"Two years, I think. Maybe three."

"And you finally got around to make an appointment to come in? You must have been so busy you didn't recognize that you were in pain."

"I didn't want to be a frivolous patient. I wanted to see if I could work it out. Or maybe it would go away by itself. Or maybe it was all in my mind."

"And — ?"

"None of the above."

It was shoulder impingement, he said. "Are you ready for the cure?"

"Depends on what the cure is."

"Well, for *normal* people, we prescribe Advil, two taken three times a day, *plus* cold packs three times a day, *and* a course of physical therapy to strengthen the long muscles that are stretching and thinning out."

The clock ticked while I waited for my doctor's comedy routine to continue.

"And then for patients who wait two years — or was that three? — to make *sure* of what they've got, we give them a cortisone shot to help break up the scar tissue they've worked so hard to build up before we send them to physical therapy."

I fixed him for being such a smart aleck. I just fainted dead away. He admitted afterward, while I was lying there with my feet elevated, that he'd never seen a patient's blood pressure drop so radically at the mere *mention* of a cortisone shot.

"I'm very suggestible," I mumbled.

But my stupid shoulder was not. Cortisone, gift of the gods that the elderly beg for to relieve the pain of age-ruined joints, gave me exactly three days of relief. The Advil-and-cold-pack routine did more to give me a self-image as an invalid than it did any ease of pain. The physical therapist got bored before I did. "Keep doing the exercises and maybe they'll help," she said unhelpfully.

The pain was a sometime thing, as if my stupid shoulder was playing hide-and-seek games with me. Some days the pain radiated down into my right hand — my *writing* hand, dammit! — and into two of my fingers. Some days I could not hold the baby quilt I was stitching or set my elbow on a car's armrest because it hurt too much. Other days were twinges of remembering, but nothing more except the hope that it had finally repaired itself. None of the nights were any good, and sleep — which was once practically a hobby of mine — dissolved into fragments.

On retreat for the holy days, I thought I cut a pretty stupid sight to the other retreatants as I sat during silent meals three times a day with a floppy ice pack slung over my shoulder that was wrapped in a dish towel and looked like a burped baby. We're reliving the agonies of Christ and Carol's got a boo-boo shoulder? On Easter morning, one of the retreatants hugged me as carefully as if she was hugging a blown-glass doll marked "fragile." She said, "I don't want to hurt your shoulder. Easter is a new beginning. Maybe it will be a fixed shoulder."

Of all my mental screwiness and twisted sinfulness that needed fixing, and the new beginning that was Easter, I had never considered physical fixing. Maybe I had reached that age. By then, seriously sleep-deprived, I was trying to convince

myself that my stupid shoulder was really the voice of an angel
that got me up in time for 5:30 a.m. vigils because I hurt too
badly to sleep.

I wanted to be suggestible enough that Lucia's words alone
(and maybe a few of her prayers on the side) would do the
trick. I hoped for an Easter miracle. I stayed the course of
Advil-icepack-exercise. I learned that hurt can turn a good
nature into a cranky one. I learned that sleep is a luxury
when you're hurting. I learned that country-western songs
may bewail the hurt of a cheatin' heart, but nobody really
cares about your stupid shoulder pain because it doesn't show
and you sound whiney.

When it hurt to hold my little ukulele, I decided I had
enough. I'll give up the gym and a good night's sleep over
to pain, but not my ukulele and attendant howling at the
moon. I found an acupuncturist nearby and signed up for a
consultation. My mother had a successful course of treatment
for arthritis pain years ago, and I'd had it to quit smoking
once, so I knew it had potential, even if my HMO didn't and
wouldn't pay for it.

I only wish the Caucasian acupuncturists (all two of them in
my experience) didn't have to spout unimaginative New Age
holistic stuff as part of their cure. Unlike psychotherapy — *so*
unlike psychotherapy — the talking cure was all coming from
the therapist instead of the patient.

"Until I was thirty-five, I had no idea of what I wanted to
be when I grew up," intoned Joe while he inserted needles
into my extremities. "Then I prayed to the Divine Life Force
and asked for wisdom, and here I am. Feeling this needle yet?"

"Yes! I'm here because I found you in the Yellow Pages.
Was that the first time you asked for wisdom or the first time
you got answers?"

"A little of both. Feeling this one yet? No? What was unusual this time I asked was the *intensity*."

Intensity in the asking or in the answers? I didn't know or try to find out. In Catholicism, which is Old Age wisdom, such intensity is the hallmark of a novena — also a Big Ask.

It's all about qi, he said, pronouncing it as "chee," the energy flowing along the meridians. If it's blocked, you can get pain — not the original, gym injury pain, but a weak spot where qi pools up, like "cancer-lite" as Joe called it.

Seven needles — two in the shoulder, one in the arm, one between my fingers, one in the foot, one in the ankle, and one between my eyes — "for good thoughts" — oh, barf, do they *have* to do that?

"This is a safe place," Joe said solemnly as he turned on the mindless tinkle music to match the water fountain that apparently comes with the New Age in a Box kit. "You'll stay in this safe place for ten minutes. It's okay to cry. Some people get very emotional."

"Fine. Is it okay to not cry?"

Bleh. I stared at the ceiling and wished I had an open mind instead of a stupid, hurting shoulder. I tried to imagine where all that stuff got stuck. The injury happened during the time I was writing my first book. The pain really started when I was working on my second book, with long hours of writing longhand exaggerating the pain. By now I was a conflicted, sleepless wreck.

My mind (which thinks it is hilarious) said, "Hey! Instead of writer's block, I got qi block!"

There was no pain when I left the bubbling fountain and gurgling acupuncturist. There was no arm. I had no awareness of my arm. Apparently I'd been living in limb awareness.

Sometimes you become your pain and acupuncture doesn't work, Joe said at the next visit. Other times, it's because there are multiple sites for the needles, and maybe you didn't get the most effective combination. People I worked with said the acupuncture worked because I *wanted* it to work. The drugs-and-surgery crowd said the cortisone hadn't worked because I *didn't* want it to.

Who knew I was so powerful? I sure didn't.

The pain returned anyway, whether I wanted it cured or not. With nothing better to do on a weekend when Felix was traveling, I marched back to the monastery "for a healing," as I called it. *Dammit, some healing, any healing, but my stupid shoulder sure would be the place to start, God, you know? And you, Blessed Joanna Mary, my patron, when do I ever ask you for anything, and is that because I'm polite or because I don't think you've got the goods, and why couldn't I get a real patron saint anyway instead of somebody I never heard of . . .*

Clearly, I was in need of some healing. The guestmaster at the monastery put me in the room across from the retreat chapel. How funny, because I planned to visit every day to ask about my poor, stupid shoulder that had become like a no-good, useless relative who won't leave and get a life, so they make yours miserable.

After the first day, I slept like a rock, which bothered me because that would get my hopes up like a prayer being answered, and we know it doesn't work like that —

We do? How does it work then?

Well, we ask, and nothing happens, and we make excuses for God so as not to embarrass Him, and also to cover our faith-butt, as it were. That's what we do. We say, *Oops, you know best, of course, and I didn't mean to imply that I knew better because I was asking about the shoulder, you know? It's okay. Thy will be done, and all that, and I know you answer, even though the answer is no, or else doesn't look like any answer I'd recognize as such. Didn't mean to put You on the spot. Hedge my bets like a bookie, I will. My ear infection is still around. Fix that, because it will go away in a day or so anyway — you'll get the credit! Okay, any healing, forgiveness for bad feelings I had during my last visit here. Okay, I'm just glad to be here no matter what, okay? And have a nice day Up There, You hear?*

Enthusiasm and activity were not enough, I read in the book I brought to entertain myself on Healing Weekend. God required more than that. He had commanded all men to *ask*, the book said.

Ask? I was not amused. Asking is hard. Asking is commitment. Asking is *not nice,* and sets you up for "no thanks, I gave at the office."

Now here's the hilarious part of the story and why I just love Catholicism and how Divine Providence is such a crackup.

Faced with my demons, between ask/don't ask, make nice to God/demand Blessed Joanna Mary earn her honors as patron to this Benedictine brat-oblate, betwixt, between, hurting and cranky, and not having a very good healing retreat as a result, I did the only thing I could think of.

I went to the monastery gift shop.

That was when the Fortune Cookie Cure Novena for a Blown Out Shoulder began, the lovely hope that I'd find an answer for sale in the monastery gift shop. And there, sitting in a rack of prayer cards that I have never seen before, and wouldn't normally bother with because I don't use prayer cards because the words are icky-gushy, and the artwork even worse, was something in the rack called, "Prayer for Wounded Shoulder."

Nah. This can't be, God, can it? Can it really? Once upon a time St. Bernard reportedly asked Jesus what his greatest unrecorded suffering was, and it was the wound in his shoulder from carrying the cross. And there came to be a prayer to this secret suffering and promises made for those who pray it, *and all you are commanded to do is to ask . . .*

I bought the prayer card. I prayed the prayer. My stupid shoulder stopped hurting. I was surprised at how much I wanted to attribute it to something else, like spontaneous all-in-my-head-and-it-went-away. I kept praying the prayer, not nine times in nine days, not any of the formula-driven ways that novenas are usually constructed. No, I prayed it every day because I found it when I was desperate, or it found me, and answers can look pretty funny if you are desperate enough to ask for them.

This church has something for everyone, even me. Christ is our life raft and sometimes you get a little piece broken off that raft, but it's all you can grab to stay afloat in a churning sea.

Why I love novenas, and why I reach for them when naked neediness rips into me, is because this church, in its graciousness, allows me to hold this tool when there are *no* tools available to fix the brokenness at hand. Our friend dying of brain cancer has the non-believers wringing their hands helplessly saying, "If there's anything I can do . . ." Another dear soul is without work and unlikely to see a job again in his field. I move heaven with my petitions to St. Peregrine and St. Joseph. The non-believers move the earth with resumes and doctors and experimental cures. Novenas allow our broken, splintered hearts a place to be poured out. *Like water, I am poured out,* says the psalmist.[10] It does not just break out, but pours out.

Novenas do not come to us with results guaranteed, no matter what the newspaper personals to St. Jude suggest. The only prayer that can be guaranteed is the one that Jesus taught. "Thy will be done." Novenas are not magic. But they give me time in prayer, and certainly it is never time wasted.

As I write this, twelve years have passed since my first novena, that super-duper, go-for-broke fifty-four-day novena. Eight of those twelve years have been smokefree, and the demon up and left with no forwarding address long ago. Once you start . . . You just never know where Grace waits its turn with you.

F I V E

The Divine Office

WHEN I BECAME a Benedictine oblate, I did so for several reasons, some more compelling than others. I wanted the sense of belonging to something, to a tradition with deep roots that would counteract the dizzying lack of permanence I felt from living in a region where neighbors moved every time property values appreciated, and earthquakes, wildfires, and rampant growth contributed to the sense of a fragile community. I wanted the *idea* of affiliating with a monastery. Twenty years ago, when I went to work at one of the top research universities in the world, I hoped that some of the intellect — they had enough of it to burn after all — would rub off on me. I hoped the same for a monastic affiliation — that their prayers, of which they had in abundance, would spill over into me.

Also, oblates went on retreat once a year together. I liked that a lot. The older I got, the fewer people I seemed to know who were willing or able to leave caretaking and family responsibilities to spend several days and nights away on a spiritual journey pit stop. I do a lot of retreats, and I loved having both a group to retreat with, and a place to retreat with them.

Of course, the final reason I became an oblate may have been the most compelling in hindsight: they invited me to join them. At the time, my spiritual dance card wasn't exactly filled to overflowing. In fact, it was empty.

So I joined up.

The retired abbot who served as oblate master and issued the invitation had his own reasons for drawing me in: he had the secret to the perfect life in God and he didn't want to keep it a secret. At first, I thought his secret must be the Rule of St. Benedict, which he pressed into my hands nearly as soon as we met. But I read it through and didn't see any secrets — or much relevance either that could come through speed-reading an old text. The Divine Office was what he called his secret, the Liturgy of the Hours, as the prayer books are actually called; the breviary as it was known in the Latin-language church before Vatican II; *Opus Dei*, the work of God, as the Benedictine Rule labeled it. It was "the prayer of the church," the old abbot explained. "Even the Pope prays it!"

That was hardly a selling point for me, Catholic not quite ten years by then and unsure that popes did much else besides travel on business a lot, pronounce things a lot, and pray a lot, hardly making them role models for me.

But the abbot was an absolute pest about the office, and eventually I gave in to praying it morning and night. It seemed to be the linchpin of oblation in his eyes, and he was the oblate master after all. There were still the other reasons on my list to satisfy my choice of being an oblate, even if the office wasn't on the list.

Truth be told, the annual oblate retreat wasn't very satisfying either, but I signed up each year anyway. It was part of what oblates did, and if I didn't, maybe that meant I wasn't an oblate anymore. It was such a slippery slope in my mind. I signed up six months in advance every year. But one particular year, I didn't have a good feeling about the retreat *before* I got there. I even called that day to confirm that there was an oblate retreat. Everything was on, everything was set to go, they said.

It was breathlessly hot, even a mile from the ocean, when I arrived. When the guestmaster checked, I was not on the retreat list after all, although I'd reserved it with the abbot in writing, as always.

"The old abbot's getting old," said the assistant guestmaster apologetically. He felt terrible because he was doing something when I called, and because he knows my name he hadn't checked reservations, just confirmed the retreat.

"He was getting old ten years ago!" I had to laugh. The abbot was ninety-four, and I expected the same from him as if he were a mere youngster of eighty-five.

The assistant found one room open, but he was pretty sure I wouldn't want it. Facing the new construction project, its picture window was completely walled over with cinder blocks. It was dark and oppressive, and promised to make me feel as if I'd been buried alive. But it *was* the oblate retreat, and I *was* an oblate, so I decided I could manage if all I did was use the room for sleeping.

When I went to unpack my car, I realized I'd have the door shut when I was sleeping, and that walled-up window wasn't going to open, and it really *would* be like being entombed, not to mention nearly ninety degrees all night. I returned the key and drove down the hot and airless hill.

It was the first retreat I would miss as an oblate. Would they miss me? Unlikely. They had each other. Would I miss them? I was unsure. I had never missed the oblate retreat before, and still wasn't sure why I went to them. The best part of making a retreat at the monastery, to me, seemed to be the opportunity to come together five times a day to pray the office. Heck, I thought, I can do that at home and still be part of the oblate retreat in spirit, and even sleep near an open window with a fan at night.

At that moment, I finally knew what the Divine Office was, and the reason for the abbot's stubborn pursuit of my praying it. It is my work of God too, my link to the monastery, the monks, the oblates, and the saints. It is the fidelity to my oblation as a Benedictine.

I finally understood another part of the Rule as I drove home on that hot night when there was no room to be an oblate on retreat. Chapter 50 of the Rule says: "Members who work so far away that they cannot return to the oratory at the proper time . . . are to perform the *Opus Dei* [Work of God] where they are. . . ."[1] As one monk, writing for oblates, explains, "Most oblates have to pray their Divine Office at home, but they are spiritually linked to their community of monks or nuns who are gathered in choir stalls to praise God in the Divine Office."[2]

Being an oblate — a lay monastic — is not about "playing monk" at the monastery, but about pulling the monastic into my world. The Divine Office is the pulley that helps me do that.

It also constitutes the largest block of chapters of Benedict's Rule for his monks. The chapter on humility is the longest chapter, and the first word of the Rule ("*Listen . . .*") may get the most press, but for boring nights when you can't sleep, let me recommend reading chapters with titles like, "How many psalms are to be said in the Night Office" (chapter 9), "How Matins is to be celebrated on Sundays" (chapter 11), or "How the Office should be performed" (chapter 19). Chapters 8–20 of the Rule's seventy-three chapters are nothing more than instructions for the Office, and further instructions are sprinkled throughout the rest of the text.

The Divine Office is composed largely of psalms, a few canticles (hymns from biblical texts), short readings from the scriptures, and intercessions.

Our prayer life is to praise and glorify God. I look at the little oratory next to my desk at home. There sits my grand-mother's cranberry glass, full of fresh-cut roses, a picture of the abbot and me, a Marian shrine I made from an oversized Altoid tin and holy cards, and the Divine Office, volume IV, ordinary time weeks 18–24. How many times have I flip-flopped from the Divine Office to something "better" for my prayer life in this past year?

It's a dry old bird, and hard chewing on nine psalms a day for the offices I pray (morning, evening, readings). Chew this: morning prayer, which I pray at 5:30 a.m., and which takes me twenty minutes (less if I'm sleepy and forget a canticle), opens with an "invitatory" asking God to open my lips to proclaim God's praise, and with Psalm 95, as Benedict suggests in his Rule (chapter 9). This is followed by two more psalms, an Old Testament canticle, a short Old Testament reading, a response, another canticle from the Old Testament (the song sung by Zechariah when his speech is returned after the birth of his son, John the Baptist[3]), the prayer intercessions, and a closing prayer. There is also an opening hymn, which I admit I have *always* ignored, out of a less-than-singing 5:30 a.m. spirit.

But it *is* 5:30 a.m. The monks at my monastery are up too, praying their first office of the day. It feels companionable and communal, even though we are separated by fifteen miles and very different lifestyles.

Evening prayer — for me usually after dinner and before going to the gym to work out — takes fifteen minutes because there's no Psalm 95 opening. There are two psalms, a short New Testament Reading, a New Testament canticle, and the Magnificat of Mary (*My soul proclaims the greatness of the Lord* . . . [4]). Finally, there are prayers of intercession and a closing prayer, as well as an ignored hymn. I don't have a singing spirit at 7:30 p.m. either.

Lastly for me is the office of readings, which can be prayed anytime, which I do immediately after evening prayer. This twenty-minute set includes three more psalms, my last ignored hymn of the day, a longish biblical reading, and a reading from the fathers of the church or the lives of the saints.

All tallied, it's nearly an hour at prayer. I am always ready to abandon the office to try something I will like "better," but fear usually brings me back. Without the office, there is no oblation. Without my Benedictine oblation, my Catholicism will fall. And then, where am I, who am I, and where am I going?

The dominoes don't *have* to fall that way, I know. There is nothing in Benedict's charter that mandates Catholicism, and indeed, it has been popularized well by non-Catholic writers like Esther de Waal (an Anglican), Kathleen Norris (a Presbyterian), and Norveen Vest (an Episcopalian). But my monastery is Catholic, and I want to partake of the Eucharist offered to my oblate community by my monastic community when I am with them physically.

Still, there are other forms of prayer quite suitable to a life attempted in Christ. As a teenager full of yearning, I prayed the morning and evening prayer found in the old Episcopal Book of Common Prayer. As a new Catholic, I used the rosary daily for quite a while until after I became a Benedictine.

Another oblate puts a good perspective on this praying of the psalms when she writes, "...but it took an affiliation with the Benedictines to lead me to a greater fidelity to prayer. While Benedictine communities frame their days around a rhythm of prayer...as an oblate it is a challenge to forge a prayer life that is both practical and persistent."[5]

It is not just oblates who face that challenge, but we seem to be the types, in general, who want to master it. My difficulty sometimes comes from being a practical sort, and not as persistent as I could be. The Divine Office was a gift to me from the abbot, on behalf of the church that prays it. It's not his fault that I find it a tough chew and don't always swallow it.

One of the early desert fathers who informed the tradition that Benedict inherited and modified agrees with me. "I think there is no labor greater than that of prayer to God," he said. For good works of any kind, perseverance will bring about results. But prayer is warfare to the last breath because our enemies, the demons, want to halt us in our heavenly journey, and turning us from prayer is their only weapon.[6]

I appreciate the endorsement of the difficulties because when it comes to demons, man, I've got 'em. They are disguised as "getting it right," and they can be absolutely vicious in torment. When the demons descend, I put away the office because it is boring, irrelevant, and the psalms all seem like boy-songs for man-God, and I am left out of the duet. There are weeks when I put away the office to do something else — *anything* else — multiple times, sometimes in a single day. There are times when I go dumpster-diving to retrieve the monthly magazine of short prayers and readings that I tossed the last time I returned to the office. Once I had to use the prayer magazine with its covers all taped back on, having torn it apart when I threw it out so I wouldn't go back and use it again — which I did anyway when the demons struck again.

Or else I decide that "art prayer" is going to be my life, and I'm at it with glue, markers, and magazine clippings at 5:30 a.m., which is great fun, but doesn't feel like prayer and doesn't connect me to anything larger than my collage diary.

"Maybe when you can't pray the office you just need to let everything sit there in front of you," advised Father Ron, a priest-friend counseling my crazies by e-mail. "Then put your hand on the books or hold the office to your heart. If you stay put and stay open with the books there, you *are* praying the office."

That has worked when I have tried it. Although it also doesn't *feel* like prayer, the demons are apparently not as perceptive as I or else slink away in boredom. Perhaps it is, however tenuous, the link I need with the community who prays the prayer of the church. "If I can pray only once a day or miss prayer altogether," writes one author, "I know that thousands of others are carrying on this living tradition for the good of all creation.... And when I actually pray the morning, afternoon, and evening hours, I know that I have taken up the call to prayer for those who did not have time or were for other reasons unable to pray."[7]

What a lovely thing: that "living tradition" she writes of was really what I sought in Catholicism, in the Benedictine charism. And I found it even if I didn't really know what it looked like.

"I always knew you were in a lonely place growing up," says my mother, which is a lovely way of saying I was a strange child, baffling to mother and child alike. "I tried different ways of parenting, but I could never reach you and bring you into safety."

I didn't know it was a lonely place when I was young. I didn't even know I was different. I was just me. But it became more evident to me in the dropping grades and increasing peer pressures in high school and college. At some point in college, I began self-medication to dull the growing pain of isolation.

Isolation is not only the birth of many an alcoholic, but frequently their death as well. I became Catholic in an affirmation of Hail Mary's aid to me in the isolation of my infirmary bed. And while the Catholic Church was my good-faith effort, it did not give me a map to get out of the lonely place.

It was the office, and my ancient abbot's insistence that I pray it at least morning and night (*"but the readings are so nice, you'll want the office of readings too — and the night office is so short . . ."*) that created a new place.

The lonely place never really disappears for the strange ones marked by genetics or inclination to travel a different road from their brothers and sisters. But the praying of the office creates another place to inhabit that is filled with the echos and spirits of all those who pray it as well. It is a daily, virtual, living community that I pick up every time I pick up the office. No matter how I come to the office — sleepy, unhappy, distracted, or even occasionally devotional — I have left the lonely place and joined the earthbound version of the heavenly host.

I imagine the best of the cloister: the Christlike abbot, not the silent ones who rarely see visitors; the open door, not the closed; the way it felt when I first went there, not the way it felt when there was no reservation, no room at the inn. Then I imagine this best part of the cloister, landing on my own doorstep twice a day like a newspaper waiting to be opened. That's what opening the Divine Office is like.

I have a bookshelf in my library filled with books by lay-people romping about monasteries, playing monk the way I once dressed up as a child and played nun. One of them is even a book I wrote. No wonder the monks' hospitality toward visitors wears thin. ("Beware of *all* visitors wearing black, carrying a notebook, and looking suitably solemn," should be a warning posted for all monastic porters.) It is a lovely idea, to think about retreats and retreating from the daily, grinding gears of life. But it is not necessarily monastic or Catholic or part of an oblate's life. The role of oblates was traditionally to enrich a devotional life, usually by praying the office. Hanging out, hanging around, and generally being a monastic pest is a more recent development, one where the boundaries between lay and professed monastics are not blurred as much as they are pushed — in the direction that goes *away* from the world.

I am one of the common sort, the one who rarely feels like she walks with God in her daily life, or talks to God in her prayers. My prayers are the mumbled, hurried kind. My *intent* in praying the office is to grow closer to God by setting aside the time to pray the prayer of the church. What it gets me is the more horizontal awareness of presence — the monks, the oblates, the saints, and yes, even the Pope, who pray the prayer — rather than any vertical sense of God "up there."

And maybe that's it. Maybe God is always and everywhere, and that includes horizontal. The office is my only way to horizontal awareness of God's presence in us and among us. The rest of the ways I pray focus more on me, or on me and Vertical God, and leave no room for anything else. The office is my rock of stability in the exhausting sea of life, upon which I crawl to rest like a drowning soul or sun myself like a simple seal twice a day. It is not cozy prayer — *you and me, God, together and holding hands!* — but the silent chant of a virtual choir of which my voice is only one part.

There is only one book that pushes the monastery into my life in the world, and that is the office. Whether I pray it, clutch it, or sing it, it is the liturgy shared with my community, the gift an elderly abbot gave me on behalf of the church, that I finally opened and decided to keep.

SIX

The Rosary

IT WAS MY FIRST PHOTO OP, and I wasn't sure what to expect. One thoughtful and funny column had already appeared in the big daily newspaper about me and the book I'd written. That had only taken breakfast with the columnist on my part. And when it comes to breakfast, I'm somewhat of an expert, having never knowingly missed one.

I was less surefooted with the local daily paper. They not only sent a reporter to interview me, but also a photographer to take a picture.

"You can use my publicity photo," I suggested. "I went to all this trouble to have a publicity shot taken just so you could use it in a situation like this." And indeed, I *had* gone to the trouble, once I got done screaming in horror at even the *idea* of a publicity shot. I had one taken when I was a music major in college that I thought looked very glamorous, if, alas, no longer much like me. Now I look like a middle-aged university lobbyist, which is exactly what I *am* — but who needs to see *that* staring back at them, particularly in black-and-white newsprint, looking like a photo negative of their *mother?*

Desperation made me crafty. It was too late for a face-lift, so I made sure my hair color was updated, and I hired the best wedding photographer I could find on the assumption that they had to make everyone look great to stay in business. Then I hired a Hollywood make-up artist who specialized in black-and-white stills. I didn't live in southern California for nothing.

The results — untouched up — looked exactly like me on the very best day of my life, like my wedding day if I'd known then what I know now. I was pleased with the result.

"My editor doesn't like posed shots," Gary said. "Too artificial."

Shoot. I did what I could remember of the make-up artist's routine and vowed not to let them talk me out of the house into the sunlight.

"Nice place," said Gary, when he arrived at my house. "The picture will look good outside."

"NO!"

I was saved by the bell when the photographer arrived. Angie was young and enthusiastic. She got there late, she said, because she stopped at our little lake and took pictures of the ducks swimming around.

"Maybe one of those photos would do for this?" I suggested politely.

They thought I was a riot. It was nerves.

"We need to frame this picture," Angie said. "The book you wrote — what was it about?"

"Well, it's about the Rule of St. Benedict. I'm a Benedictine oblate, and I thought I would sit in this chair holding up a copy of the Rule of St. Benedict. I have it right here... "

"My editor won't like that," Gary jumped in. "She'll see a picture of an author holding a book. She doesn't like that."

I was beginning to develop distaste for this editor, but Angie tried to be helpful. "This rule . . . okay, by St. Somebody, right? You wrote a book about a saint?"

"Sort of. You see, St. Benedict wrote this Rule, he called it, a spiritual way of life . . . "

"Ah, so it is a Catholic book you wrote. . . . "

"Well, not exactly. St. Benedict dates back to the late fifth century before there were schisms in the church. . . . "

"Okay," said Angie, obviously not willing to let me dampen her enthusiasm for her work, this beautiful day, those wonderful photos she'd just taken of ducks on the lake. "So let me think a minute . . . " She put her hand up to her chin and gazed at me. "Catholic. Catholic. We need you to look Catholic."

"And just how the *hell* am I supposed to do that?" This was not going well, not at all.

She pondered another moment and then lit up. "I know! Beads! They have those beads! Do you have some of those beads somewhere?"

It had just gotten a lot worse. As I went to fetch rosary beads, I protested. "Lots of Catholics don't even use these anymore."

"Oh! My grandmother had them! She used them all the time!"

So there was my peer group to Angie. Grandmotherly, and all those grandmothers carried rosary beads in their pocket for a quick fix. Now, *my* grandmother was of Northern Irish descent, defiantly Protestant, and would have responded to dangling rosary beads like a vampire to a crucifix.

But there was no arguing with Angie. She fussed me into the chair, began draping the rosary around my hands in artistic arrangements that could have never survived actually praying them, and began clicking away with her camera like I was a duck swimming on a pond.

"Dammit, no!" I finally said. "This doesn't work. It will offend people. Rosaries are private prayers." I turned to Gary, who was leafing through my magazines waiting to begin the interview. "Your editor won't want offensive pictures."

"Oh no," he said. "She won't want that."

They ended up with a photograph of one very unhappy author looking off into the distance, wishing she was anywhere else as she strummed her ukulele. It got a lot of attention, that photo, maybe as much as one of me dangling rosary beads in clearly unusable positions would have, looking very "Catholic."

It might be less true now, but when I was growing up, Catholics, if not grandmothers, were known for their rosaries. It truly looked like "what Catholics do" to those of us who were not Catholic. Rosaries were what Catholics kept bedside or in their car, and Protestants looked on them with a mixture of ignorance and fear, maybe thinking this was part of the superstitions Catholics held to. I know even in 1990, my RCIA class looked lively one day when we were asked by the deacon if we had questions about becoming Catholics in a few weeks.

"When do we get our rosaries?" asked one woman in her twenties. I guess she thought they got issued, like dog tags, to incoming Catholics. I could afford to feel smug because I already *had* mine and had looked up in a book how to pray it. When I imparted this information to the rest of my class, they were insanely jealous, like I had just gotten extra credit.

Unlike the Rule of St. Benedict that got me in trouble with the photographer, praying the rosary only goes back to the Middle Ages, when an enthusiastic Dominican preacher, Alan de Rupe, preached the story of a vision given to St. Dominic. In the vision, St. Dominic was given the rosary by Mary as a prayerful means of involving her assistance.

Long before any such vision or its popularization, monks used beads to count the 150 psalms they chanted in their

Liturgy of the Divine Office. And other religious traditions, including Muslims and Buddhists, use strings of beads to count off prayer repetitions or to finger as worry beads. ("You'd love Thailand," Felix reported back mischievously after a solo adventure there. "More people with beads than here! You'd be right at home. Incense too!")

Over time, the Dominican version became the popular "people's choice" with its decades of Hail Marys, bookended by Our Fathers and Glory Be's, and set into meditative "chapters" of holy mysteries: the Joyful, the Sorrowful, the Glorious moments in the life of Mary, the death of Jesus, and the life everlasting for all. It was this version that was known as Our Lady's Psalter.

The rosary had been developed as a substitute for praying the psalms. As a form of private and public worship, the psalms probably go back furthest in our Judeo-Christian heritage. Some are written as early as the fifth century BC, and the majority were composed for liturgical use. As a Jew, Jesus would have prayed them daily, and their words were on his lips even at the hour of his death.

St. Benedict takes great pains to lay out the Psalter over the hours of liturgy his monks pray. An indication of the centrality of the psalms to a monk's life comes at the end of a chapter on the order of psalms to be chanted. St. Benedict tells us:

> No matter what, all 150 psalms must be chanted during the week so that on Sunday Matins the series may start afresh. Monks who chant less than the entire Psalter, with canticles, each week are slothful in their service to God. Our spiritual fathers performed with determination in one day what we now take a whole week to do.[1]

The slouches! Even in the twelfth century, we find the sterling examples of saints such as St. Lambert, who not only served as bishop of Vence, France, but also exhibited extraordinary humility, miraculous healings (especially in restoring sight to the blind), *and* for his last thirty years, recited the entire Psalter every day.[2] He must have found his heavenly reward exceptionally restful after all that recitation.

The problem was literacy. Because many monks and most laity couldn't read, a substitute for the 150 psalms was constructed. The Liturgy of the Hours, or Divine Office, follows a liturgical year, beginning with Advent and concluding with Pentecost. So the mysteries of the rosary and the prayerful repetitions of shorter prayers substituted for the psalms, constituting a miniature Divine Office. It's our office, we who are not monks. Even to pray it alone joins us in spirit with all the others in the world who pray this way, just as praying the office unites a Benedictine oblate like me in spirit with the monastic community I am affiliated with.

I don't pray the rosary every day, although I love praying it. One of the many gifts I found in Catholicism that I never found in other churches was a prayer life so laden in sacramentals, just *lousy* with them. Although I was an Episcopalian growing up — a church which can hold the possibility of the sacramental and sensual in worship — my own local worship was of the plain Protestant vanilla type. I approached the Catholic Church like a kid in a spiritual penny-candy store who'd just been given a *whole dollar* to spend.

It was the Franciscans at a nearby mission who showed me around the candy store. They were a joyous lot, determined to share the goodies of the faith. At every retreat or day of recollection with them, there was a feast of goodies, most of them new to me. It was there at the mission that I first experienced the Exposition of the Blessed Sacrament, stations of the cross, centering prayer, and iconic prayer.

"Which is the best, do you figure?" we'd ask, so nervous about getting it *right* or at least *better,* whether we were born Catholics or immigrants right off the convert boat.

"They're all ways to God," the retreat director would say, practically coming out of his sandals for joy. "Pick one. Try them all. It's a buffet of prayer choices."

"I'll have what *he's* having," I would mutter to whoever was sitting next to me. I didn't know what Franciscans "did" for a prayer life, but the retreat director sure seemed happy about it.

What I loved about the rosary was that it was tactile. My prayer life could rest in my hands instead of being processed through the printed page. I've always felt that stitching can be a very prayerful activity. It's repetitious, but the repetitions build up a body of material — in my case, embroidered baby quilts. I stitch and stitch, hour upon hour of little *x*'s, and my thoughts drift to the mother who will receive the quilt, if I know who that is, or to Hail Mary if I don't. The Pope has said of the rosary that it has "a peaceful effect on those who pray it," and leads them to see the face of Christ in others.[3]

So does stitching. Sometimes I think my best prayer life is in my hands.

It is also on my tombstone, or actually the niche where Felix's and my ashes will be interred. When I purchased the niche, I wanted the names, dates of birth, and any optional engraving done *then,* just to be tidy and organized. My Christmas shopping is complete before Labor Day. My burial niche was purchased before I was forty-five years old. I'm just like that: no wonder Catholicism's "smells and bells" were such an overwhelming, if messy, experience. Since Felix had *no* interest in the entire Last Apartment Project, as I named it — and I can't imagine why he didn't care, since it means we will never have to move again — I had a carved rosary draped around our niche names.

I mentioned the eagerness of the RCIA class to get rosaries as their rightful due in becoming Catholics. I wasn't waiting on any rosary fairy to leave one under my pillow while I slept. I had begun pawing through the Yellow Pages under "Church Supplies" after two months of formal instruction into the Catholic Church. I was ready to go straightaway to the good stuff.

Charlotte, a faculty member I worked with, who was also a convert to Catholicism, was a little annoyed at my determination to buy myself a rosary plus anything else that struck my faith-fancy. "Faith is not about buying things," she would lecture. "You need to be learning more about the church, not siphoning off your desire for God into shopping for holy stuff."

Whoa! — did I have a desire for God or did I just want a rosary because it would prove I was becoming a Catholic and I needed proof? Well, both, probably, and it showed on my face when I got Charlotte's lecture.

Charlotte showed up at my desk the next day and handed me a rosary. "This is for you," she said. "You don't just look at it; you have to pray with it. It is not a piece of jewelry; it is an object of respect. You treat it like an invitation Jesus sent you to talk to his mother."

I looked at the beads, my first rosary, which she laid on my desk. There were small black beads that looked like little pebbles on a chain of uneven links. A crucifix hung on one end, also small and dark brown. I hated brown and black together. I was disappointed: this wasn't pretty. I wanted rosary beads that were *pretty.*

I'm sure my face gave away my secret thoughts because Charlotte started up again. "This is not about buying holy stuff. This is about prayer. You don't know who had these before you — maybe they were the comfort of an old lady before she died who will be praying for you too because you've got her beads and become her sister in Christ . . . "

I admit it. I was a spiritual brat. I didn't want an unknown sister in Christ praying for me. I wanted nice, pretty rosary beads.

"I had the priest there bless them," Charlotte said. "Now you *use* them."

"Thank you, Charlotte. You're too good to me." As soon as she left, I told my boss I had errands to run, and ran off to the church supply store. There I found a lovely crystal rosary, heavy in my hands, that sparkled and reflected the light. I bought it and brought it home. I'm ashamed to say I don't know what became of the one Charlotte so kindly scrounged up for me. I hope it didn't *really* belong to an old woman's last comfort because she'll be out to get me for this.

I didn't know that rosaries (or crucifixes, or other holy objects) could be blessed by a priest. That was probably in the advanced part of the *Catechism,* I figured. When I got to that part and my fellow catechumates got *their* standard-issue rosaries, I'd find out more.

We never did cover rosaries in RCIA, which disappointed a lot of us. I bought a pamphlet for fifteen cents and used it to learn how to say the rosary. I never learned the mysteries by heart. I had enough to learn the Hail Holy Queen prayer at the end. But I pasted the pictures portraying each mystery into the front and back flaps of the brand-new Catholic Bible that I'd also purchased and looked at the images when I said the rosary. That is: I looked at the images when I wasn't looking

at how the light refracted off the faceted-glass rosary beads
and made such pretty lights...

When my Auntie Blanche died, I asked if I could have
something of hers, preferably Catholic. For if my mother and
her people were of the staunch Northern Irish and English
Protestant sort, my father's people were all papist Frenchmen.
The Reformation lived and relived itself with my little family.

A box came back to me by mail. "This rosary was in your
aunt's hands at the wake," my mother wrote. "It looked so
pretty against the purple dress of hers that I picked for her to
wear when she was laid out."

Obviously, my love of pretty rosaries comes from my Protestant mother, matching one to a dress for a dead woman.
And it *was* pretty: purple beads, each encased in a filigree
casement of delicate gold, a good-sized crucifix on the end.
I never used it: the filigree made it impossible to slide from
one bead to the next and the chain had worn so much with
age and possibly use that the decades had begun to slip into
each other. But this one had belonged to a real old lady, a
family member in a family small in numbers, and it had probably been her comfort, so I treat it with respect for all of those
reasons. She would find it amusing. At my Episcopal christen-
ing, my parents were allowed three godparents, two of whom
would be the same sex as the baby. Auntie Blanche had been
the Catholic godmother of my two godmothers. And now,
Catholic, I had inherited her beads.

For a year, I worked closely with a student political organization on campus. Their politics and intentions rarely matched
official university policy or intention, but we worked hard together in a difficult year, and I was both sad and proud to
watch their graduation.

A month after the graduation, the student leader showed up at my office with a gold-plated finger rosary in a bag that read, "Oggetti Religiosi, Città del Vaticano."

"We were traveling in Europe for our graduation present," she said, "and when we got to the Vatican, we all thought of you, since you're the only Catholic we know. We had it blessed and everything."

I'd been blessed by them already. On a lobbying trip to Sacramento with the group of students, I'd borrowed the car we used to drive there together so I could go to Mass on Sunday before an all-day meeting. Despite their staying up all Saturday night to party, while I was sleeping in another part of the hotel in a room whose number I refused to reveal, they all showed up in the hotel lobby, bleary-eyed but showered, to attend Mass with me. Their mothers would have probably fainted had they known, but it was always our secret. The finger rosary is special. It's been blessed, and it tucks into the palm of my hand as I move it around my finger on the really bad, comfortless days, the days when the repetitions of Hail Marys are better than Prozac for a repetitious, obsessive, nail-biting mind like mine.

One Easter retreat at the monastery felt particularly lonely and difficult. My room was isolated from the daily comings and goings, the fellow retreatants seemed to be in various sorts of isolating distress, and my beloved abbot was wheelchair-ridden because of a broken knee. The weather was raw and nasty, and I wanted to go home the entire time.

Somehow I stuck it out, and decided to reward myself with a new rosary. I have never cured myself of buying holy stuff, and doubtless it siphons away from what I really desire, which is Christ. It also, possibly, crosses over into idolatry, although I know it isn't the possession of holy stuff that makes me holy or not. *You have to use the items for their intended purposes, Carol . . .*

Well, I was going to use this rosary because I was going to find the perfect one, dammit, and I was going to have it blessed and everything, just like a real Catholic would do, just like I'd seen busloads of pilgrims spilling into the bookstore do. The monastery always had a priest-monk on call for bookstore blessings, and the cashier kept a vial of holy water and cloth next to her cash register for those occasions.

I chose a rosary of smooth round wooden beads because the wood reminded me of the cross of Christ. The crucifix was small, but had embedded the Medal of St. Benedict. The medal is much loved and revered by Benedictines, and its powers as a sacramental are attributed to the merits of Christ Crucified, so its placement in the crucifix seemed highly appropriate.

"Could I get this blessed?" I asked at the register. It was a big, nervy, CATHOLIC question for me. I'd never asked. The holy items in my Catholic wardrobe that had been blessed had appeared in my life that way through the requests of others.

"Sure," the cashier said and picked up the phone for the priest on bookstore call.

There was no answer.

"He's probably hearing a confession," she said. "Come back later."

I didn't. I was too embarrassed, and it probably wasn't important anyway — just some old Catholic custom or something — and it's about prayer. *Use it, Carol.*

I did. Not every day, because as a Benedictine oblate, my primary daily prayer is the office, rather than this "laity" office. But it is the comfort of my hands, and it seems more important to me as I get older. It's a public prayer I can join in at special

times and sad times. It's a private prayer I sometimes share
when I'm in the retreat chapel on retreat at the monastery
and the old abbot, my much-loved spiritual advisor, slips in
the side door to say his beads too in the companionable silence
of the Blessed Sacrament.

My courage takes a long time to come to a boil on a lot of
things Catholic. I have the uncertainty of the convert, the one
who picked the team to play on, not the one who was picked.
Three years after I bought the Benedictine rosary, when it
hadn't been supplanted by a "better," more perfect one, and
was beginning to feel like I was holding Christ's invitation to
talk to Hail Mary in my hands, I came to the monastery for
confession. Before I go to confession, I will write notes of sins
so I won't back down from admitting them or suddenly forget
them. At the end of this list, I wrote "get rosary blessed."

The abbot was delighted to see it, and probably to see me
with it as well. "The Benedictine one gets its own blessing,"
he said. "It's a very long blessing." I had all the time of eternity. I watched him gather up the beads in his ancient hands
and with deep reverence and respect, he carefully blessed the
object of my hands' life of prayer. In so doing, the blessing, like
the holy water he used, splashed a little on the user as well.

With such strong ties to the history of the laity of the
church, and rooted in the memory of those dear addicted
saints rattling off 150 psalms a day for years, or the monks in
the Divine Offices, or Christ in his prayer, it made me down-
right cranky when Pope John Paul II created and encouraged
a new set, the Luminous Mysteries of Light. It throws off the
symmetry and history built around the 150 psalms, although
I know very few people who would pray the complete rosary
daily, and I would consider that on par with chanting all 150
psalms in a day.

What was he thinking? There was some commentary written at the time of the new mysteries that the Pope was offering a corrective to accusations that the rosary is "too Marian" in its focus, that he was trying to bring the full scriptural story into focus. But the Pope loves Mary, loves the rosary, AND declared his twenty-fourth year as Pope to be a Year of the Rosary. So why was he *really* messing with it?

Plus there was the problem of where to put these mysteries now that we've got them. Traditionally, the Joyful Mysteries were prayed on Monday and Thursday, the Sorrowful on Tuesday and Friday, and the Glorious "won" with Wednesday, Saturday, and Sunday. It took some shuffling to get the Luminous into the rotation once (on Thursdays), reduce the Glorious to twice a week (Sunday and Wednesday), and shuffle the Joyful to Monday and Saturday.

Not scheduled in anything I have read were the block mystery seasons. If the rosary is like a miniature Divine Office, it also followed some of the intensity of the office around significant liturgical times. My four-volume office takes up so much space because one volume focuses on the office for the Advent/Christmas season, and one volume, the largest of the set, focuses on the Lent/Easter season. The remaining two volumes cover ordinary time.

So too, its miniature had its focuses. From Advent to Christmas, you could recite the Joyful Mysteries daily; during Lent, you would recite the Sorrowful Mysteries until you were practically breathing with them; and from Easter to Pentecost you would pray the Glorious.

The Luminous turned every day into ordinary day, and that made me grumpy. Why it even changed was another kind of mystery, ecclesiastical, and therefore beyond me. I wasn't consulted. I planned to ignore it.

Can you meditate on the mysteries and pray the rosary at the same time? The rosary involves repetition, but it is meant to be meditative, a springboard to contemplation.

"I was brought up Catholic, in a very devout family," Hildegard, my oblate-class buddy once told me. "Our family gathered around the fireplace every Sunday night and prayed the rosary together. It is such a beautiful memory of my family to look back on. I should pray the rosary all the time. But I don't like it — all the mysteries, the counting, the beads, the boredom — not my kind of prayer."

Catholic novelist Flannery O'Connor wrote in a letter to a fellow Catholic, "If I attempt to keep my mind on the mysteries of the rosary, I am soon thinking about something else, entirely nonreligious in nature."[4]

Meditation has received a lot of attention in recent years, especially as baby boomers bring the practices from their past into the Catholic mainstream. And contemplative prayer is big stuff nowadays as well with its "centering prayer." If I need a guaranteed recipe for falling asleep, centering prayer is my ticket. Apparently my center needs a pillow and a nap. And meditation is my ticket out, from good intentions and lofty ideals, to wondering what to wear to work tomorrow, and did my husband really say to me what I *think* he said?

The riches in Catholicism for me lie in its history, in the diversity of prayer life and practices, in the abundance of Holy Spirit that splashes up a little on the users of its tools. The rosary is my handle to meditating on Christ. Even Flannery O'Connor wrote later to the same friend, noting that she prayed the rosary on the friend's behalf and stayed awake for the whole thing. "Very unusual," she noted. "The rosary is at least tangible."[5]

Tangible, yes, and also surprisingly contemporary with or without a face-lift. The mysteries modeled in the scriptures — joyful, sorrowful, glorious — can also be seen today.

Felix's friend was dying of cancer. On one particularly difficult visit, Felix sat at his friend's bedside and told him he loved his friend, while the wife of the dying man and I sat at a piano and sang "Memories" together. The caretaker thought Duane would die "soon." The wife measured that as a week. Felix said it looked at most to be forty-eight hours.

I went to church early that Saturday night and decided to pray the rosary for Duane. I used the Sorrowful Mysteries because it seemed to match my mood, and learned it is easier to approach the Lord's suffering when you have a living example of one of his creatures going through suffering as well —

The First Sorrowful Mystery, the Agony in the Garden: Duane received news of the brain tumor, the cruel fate that had his name on it. Remove it, he said. We're going to fight this thing, said his wife. The experimental treatments began. They tried to outrun it.

The Second Sorrowful Mystery, the Scourging at the Pillar: The tumor came back, whispered his wife while she wept on the telephone. Had it ever left? But now the experiments had failed and the options were gone, and the painful reality lashed at all of us, but most of all Duane.

The Third Sorrowful Mystery, the Crowning with Thorns: There's nothing now we can do, said the doctors. It's official. You're dead. We're not sure of the date, but it won't be long now.

The Fourth Sorrowful Mystery, the Carrying of the Cross: He fell in the night. She called Security to help him up. He fell again. And again. Sometimes he fell three times in the night because he got up and forgot where he was. Or he got up and thought he was well. Now there are three women carrying his final burden. He can no longer stand under its weight at all.

The Fifth Sorrowful Mystery, the Crucifixion: He's on morphine now all the time, and oxygen. He no longer eats or drinks, but deep inside he worries for his wife when he's gone. For himself he is no longer worried. It is finished. The women minister to him, the angels sing, and everybody holds their breath and awaits his last, tortured breaths.

He died an hour after we left, sometime between the Fourth and Fifth Sorrowful Mystery, and I knew that saying the rosary would never be an easy contemplation exercise again. This time, I lived it.

So why did the offering of the Luminous Mysteries make me cranky? The mysteries themselves have been around and meditated on and contemplated for thousands of years. Pope John Paul only arranged them around the rosary for our use.

They are clunky, without resonance, I think, when I hear the daily Mass's faithful few pray them for the first time. They are prayed with one eye on cheat notes, hardly from the heart.

But the faithful have begun to weave them into the warp and woof of time. Someday, somewhere, an artist will begin a series of paintings in acrylics or watercolors or pastels, suitable mediums for luminous mysteries. Meditations will sprout up like weeds around these flowers. These new mysteries will begin to resonate from associations made from time and prayers. And ours will be the first hands that fold them over into time and eternity.

Adoration

"**W**E HAVE PITIFUL ADORATION at my church," my aunt on the Catholic side of the family said. I'd never heard of a pitiful adoration. It sounded like a particular kind, like Sorrowful Mysteries or stations of the cross.

"What's a pitiful adoration?" I asked, always interested in variations on a noble theme.

"Nobody shows up when they sign up!"

Oh. *That* kind of pitiful, as in pathetic.

I am so fortunate that the parish where I belong, thanks wholly to Karen's determined efforts and Father Don's willingness, has a twenty-four-hour adoration of the Blessed Sacrament once a month. It is my taste of something that was once far more common in the church.

Catholics coming of age in the last twenty-five years or so, and the converts like me, who have slipped into the back of the church since the 1980s, do not share in the collective memories of celebration of the Feast of Corpus Christi and forty hours devotions, or the quieter observance of Eucharistic exposition, perpetual adoration, or the making of a holy hour. These practices and celebrations were popularized and formalized from the Middle Ages onward. They were ways to allow the faithful to appreciate the mystery of the Eucharist and to increase their desire to participate in the Mass when the Eucharist is actually consumed in community. They were the practices developed for and loved by the common worshipper who could not understand the theology of prayers of consecration, particularly as they were then prayed in Latin, by a priest with his back to the congregation.

In the Middle Ages some people would run from church to church on a Sunday morning, just to catch the moment when the Host and chalice were raised after consecration. This vision of Christ present would, it was believed, prolong youthfulness and prevent eye diseases. Eucharistic devotions encouraged you to stick around awhile, to anticipate and desire full Communion.

When I see, every week, the number of people pouring into the back half of the church barely in time for the Gospel reading, and exiting as soon as they've gotten their goodies (Communion), I wonder if there's been much progress spiritually since the Middle Ages superstitions. And there seems to be some official sanctioning of that attitude. "In the light of our own renewed understanding of the communal nature of the Eucharist," writes a professor of theology, "it would be as incongruous now to have benediction immediately following Mass as it would be for a chef to emerge from the kitchen after dinner and walk among the restaurant patrons, showing off the entrées that the customers had just consumed." Then, just in case you still had your fingers on the edge of the centuries of a devotion once much loved, he slams the window shut on them: "Jesus left us the Eucharist to be eaten, not adored."[1]

I wouldn't dream of arguing theology with the learned. I am probably closer to my Middle Ages brethren in simple-minded faith that sometimes borders, I am sure, on the superstitious.

So I will only suggest that Jesus didn't intend the Eucharistic table to serve fast food — all meal, no desire.

A different professor of theology, writing in a different publication, suggests that adoration can become an occasion that lets the heart of the Mass, "our encounter with the risen Jesus in the sacramental signs of bread and wine, and in the sacramental narrative of God's saving history," be the object of our continued thought and gaze, inviting us into deeper participation in the Eucharistic meal.[2]

The Catholic Church did not throw out the baby with the bathwater, as my father was fond of saying, with its massive reformation called Vatican II. The devotion it provided of adoration is still available, and the revised *Catechism* still claims that "to visit the Blessed Sacrament is . . . a proof of gratitude, an expression of love, and a duty of adoration toward Christ our Lord."[3]

The trick for the newcomers is to find it.

On a five-day silent retreat at a Franciscan mission, I was treated not just to the Eucharistic meal daily, but to a whole banquet of devotions unknown to me. "For those of you who've missed benediction and exposition, we decided to offer that to you tonight," said Father Rusty in his usual joyous way, like this was the greatest treat in the universe, and who *wouldn't* want to indulge?

I got suckered in by his joyfulness, as well as the murmurs of homesickness from the older retreatants, who clearly had been missing something I'd never heard of or seen. When I joined up in the retreat chapel with everybody after the last official meditation, Father Rusty emerged, fully robed in liturgical splendor with Brother Ruffino incensing every step. The little congregation sang from memory, *O salutaris hostia, Quae caeli pandis ostium . . .* (O Saving Victim, op'ning wide /

The gate of heav'n to us below!) I didn't know the song or anything else going on. I'd never seen a monstrance before, but it looked like Father Rusty was holding the San Diego sun above his head and then setting it on the altar for all of us to behold.

I stayed for an hour. I wasn't certain what real Catholics bring to adoration, so I brought my Bible just in case. As the retreatants settled into their prayer books or looked at the monstrance, I knew I had to do *something* or else fall asleep. I opened my Ignatius Bible and Psalm 62 beckoned me: *For God alone my soul waits in silence.*[4] What a nice verse, ten little clip-clop syllables that even I, with the attention span of a flea, could hold onto for a moment or two.

In God alone, my soul waits . . . Clip-*clop,* clip-*clop,* clip-*clop-*clop. I watched the candlelight reflect and refract off the monstrance and played my fingers to the gentle rhythm of my new psalm-song. I'd forgotten my watch, which was probably a good thing, given my time-clock mentality. I slid into timelessness. Maybe that's another word for eternity. I got to rest in the Lord forever — or until Father Rusty took the monstrance away, whichever came first. *In God alone . . .* clip-*clop,* clip-*clop . . .*

A story is told of a priest who saw a young man spending hours in front of the tabernacle, where the Blessed Sacrament resides. "What do you do all this time?" he asked.

And the young man answered, "I let my soul enjoy the sunshine."[5] I am a great one for taking naps and falling deeply asleep only to awake deeply refreshed ten minutes later. Adoration does that to me from inside out.

After the introductory offer from the Franciscans, I didn't see anything about holy hours or adoration for several years.

The monks at my Benedictine monastery keep two taberna-
cles with the consecrated Host available: one at their little
abbey church and one at their *tiny* retreat chapel. The tiny
retreat chapel is available twenty-four hours a day, and I began
to stop in for brief visits when I was at the monastery for retreats or oblate visits. I would even spend hours there writing
when I felt too uncomfortable or too alone writing elsewhere.
Hardly adoration, but those quick visits reminded me of that
one hour with Christ at the mission, and served in a way to
acquaint me with this particular way of knowing him. It became an acquired joy, rather than a thunderstruck awareness.
My Benedictine abbot would give as penance the instruction
to spend time in the presence of the Blessed Sacrament after
hearing confessions — even as he assured me it was hardly
"penance" to do such. It became an acquired sense of Presence and a marvelous focus for meditative prayer in a restless
soul such as mine.

As one writer puts it, "Prayer is always an encounter with
Mystery, but it seems more obvious to me, as I pray before
the Blessed Sacrament, that the Lord is there, and that in the
stillness of a little room, I am somehow at the heart of the
church."[6]

Karen was determined to bring adoration to my parish. At
least, thanks to monks and friars, I knew what it was and
signed on. She didn't get permission for perpetual adoration,
which was her goal (and probably still is), but she did get
permission to stretch our standard treatment of the first Friday of each month — morning mass, benediction, exposition
until 4:00 p.m., reposition — to a twenty-four-hour exposition lasting until First Saturday's morning Mass. I took the
5:00 a.m. hour, along with a few others, and was amazed to
find, when I got there at 4:45 a.m. on a Saturday morning,

that ten or so people had been there, watchers of the night, praying, reading, adoring — not a sleeper in the group.

Who *were* these people? Our priest worried that benediction until 4:00 p.m. had been a struggle to maintain, and here were people from midnight onward, seeking out the Lord where he might be most visibly found. Some of the people there I recognized over time as the core faithful, who attended daily mass in that same chapel. Others were like me, perhaps day workers who could not attend a morning mass or a daytime exposition, but who *could,* if offered, give up an hour of a weekend night to be with their Lord. It was like slipping out of the house on a secret date, a hidden rendezvous. I loved it.

Notes in the back of a prayer book I carried: *Fourth of July, holiday weekend, 2002, getting up at 3:15 a.m. voluntarily. Hiroko's mother is dying, and they've brought in hospice. Can you do her hour at 4:00 a.m. instead of yours at 5:00?*

Of course. The adorers have filled in around my travels, and now it's my turn. Three-fifteen arrives in the dead of the night. Off and on during my short sleep, I wake up and think of them, the silent faithful, taking their turns to be with Christ in the little day chapel. They have been coming and going since Friday morning's mass concluded. At 3:15 a.m. when the alarm finally goes off, I think of Hiroko. She must surely be awake, too, in the dark night and agony shared with the dying.

This one's for Hiroko.

She enters the chapel right behind me. She is dressed in a dark dress instead of the usual 4:00 a.m. jeans I see her in when we trade places. Her face is puffy. Before she takes her seat, she goes over to one of the 3:00 a.m. people getting ready to leave and whispers. I hear the other person whisper back, I am so sorry. *Hiroko takes an end seat and kneels. She puts her head in her hands and takes up her tissue. She kneels the whole hour, weeping and looking toward the monstrance on the altar.*

What a place to be when your mother has just died! I think. And then, what better place to be . . .

I do not feel particularly devotional this morning, nor do I have any particular sense of Presence as I normally do. Mostly I am in awe of the ordinariness of these people, gathering themselves up in the dead of the night — before even the newspaper man is up! — for this extraordinary opportunity we Catholics sometimes have to spend an hour or two in the presence of our beloved Lord. And while I have never seen myself in the devotions of chanting monks, nor in the good works of busy-bee ministries, here in the very Presence of great love and ordinary goodness, I feel at home among family: living, dying, adoring, weeping, awaiting daybreak.

We settled down to a regular, once-a-month cycle of adoration at church, and the crowds dwindled after the first few months as crowds always do. But the steady faithfulness of the regulars was so touching in all the steadfast, private love, and I have tried to stay as much a part as my travel schedule permits.

When it does not permit adoration, it still allows quick visits. As a lobbyist, my business travel is an unglamorous rut, usually to the state capitol in Sacramento. During one such trip when politics were particularly difficult and the politicians likewise, I spent my late lunch hour in the side chapel of the Cathedral of the Blessed Sacrament. In early morning hours of adoration, I might pray or read. Here, this time, with the ugly pulsations of a body politic gone screwy outside, I found company and quiet inside and just sat in it.

Plus *nobody* in my day job would *ever* stumble onto me *here.*

Sometimes I feel like my love of adoration is an escape from that screwy world I work and live in. I can take comfort that Mother Teresa, known for her activism, insisted that adoration occupy the center of her sisters' daily work. She felt that adoration of Christ was a dark way, dark love. "To all appearances he is absent . . ." she writes, "so faith must supply what is lacking to our feeble senses."[7]

Isn't that lovely? I always feel like I am taking the lazy way of adoration, like a Mary, when the world is so in need of Marthas.

Remind me about the lazy part when the alarm goes off this Saturday of another holiday weekend at 3:00 a.m. I offered to fill in for any hour of adoration that had a holiday "hole" in it. Karen called me an "angel" — for me, that's a first — and gave me the 4:00 a.m. slot again. Whether it's an old-fashioned devotion or not, there is nothing I would rather do than to get up in the middle of the night, pull on a long dress and sandals, and slip away for a secret date with Christ. *He is always with me when I call.* Sometimes it is good to be the one who comes when *he* calls — *So you could not keep watch with me for one hour?*[8]

Hiroko and her friend are there when I arrive. She sits in utter devotion while he reads from his Bible.

After First Friday Mass yesterday morning, we all filed out behind Father Don and squeezed through the narrow hall to the day chapel. It felt like Palm Sunday and all of us were proclaiming, We're with him . . . We filed into the chapel that Diane had just dressed like a bride in white roses from her garden, and you wanted to cry for the sense of community you had.

Now, returning in the stretch of night before daybreak, the silence is like that of the tomb. So this is what Holy Saturday was like when they all left to pick up the pieces of their shattered lives and dreams. The silence almost hurts your ears. I don't think I ever quite realized before that love and presence work both ways...

EIGHT

Holy Days of Obligation

THE FRENCH-CANADIAN FAMILY of my college boyfriend celebrated more than *my* French-Canadian side of the family did, so I knew where to hang out when the holidays rolled around. Anybody could celebrate New Year's Eve, but Ronald and his family *started* there, and continued until late into New Year's Day and evening. It was certainly an effective way to buy time before the resolutions kicked in — if you could still remember them post-celebration.

The image I still have in my mind after all these years is from one New Year's Day, just before it turned dark, when the old ladies left the party behind. We'd been drinking and carousing for hours and hours by then, and the thin light that passed for winter sun was already caving in to early nightfall. It had never warmed up enough during the day to soften the glazed-ice roads, and, all around, the conditions were perfect to stay where you were and party for a few more hours — except for the old ladies.

Suddenly, as if by prearranged signal, Ronald's grandmother and aunt announced it was time to go, and began the laborious process of layering up clothes and footwear against the cold and ice outside. It can be as tough to dress the elderly when body parts are stiff and reluctant as it is to dress infants when body parts are rubbery. Plus the old ladies were getting quite tipsy from hours of homemade wine, nibbling on sweets instead of real food, and sitting instead of getting some activity. Once they got up, they discovered they were pretty wobbly. Rather than help, the rest of us allowed ourselves to be entertained by the spectacle and the grunts, giggles, and mild curses that accompanied the show.

Lipsticks were applied, a little lopsidedly, noses were powdered, and grey locks were pressed under the Sunday pillbox felt-covered hats with black lace veils attached. Finally the old ladies were ready to leave. Off they went down the icy street, clutching each other by the elbow to keep from falling, unsteady with wine within and ice without.

As we all watched them slipping down the street through our view from the parlor window, I said, "Where on *earth* are they going?" For nobody had asked them, and everybody seemed to know but me what was going on.

"To church," said Ronald's mother, sounding somewhat exasperated. "If they don't fall and break their legs first."

Church? On New Year's *Day*? Now I'd heard everything. I might have been French-Canadian on my father's side, but it was my mother's English-Northern-Irish-Protestant side that brought us all to church each week. Couldn't these Catholics get enough of it? Wasn't it bad enough how they all dragged off each Sunday no matter how much the Saturday night before intruded?

"It's a holy day of obligation," Ronald's mother explained seeing my look. "That's why." She said it like a chant: *holydayofobligation,* and I didn't understand. The way her mouth tightened when she said it, I didn't ask for clarification, or why, if the old ladies were obligated, she and the rest of the Catholic revelers weren't also obligated.

In fact, what the Western calendars celebrate as New Year's, the church celebrates as the Solemnity of Mary, Mother of God, formerly called the Feast of the Circumcision. Christmas began to be celebrated on December 25 in the 400s, and the Circumcision was then counted eight days later, as Jewish law would have dictated. It must have always been a difficult holy day of obligation to maintain once the Gregorian calendar named January 1 as the beginning of the new year. In the times when paganism dominated, the orgies of festivities crowded and contrasted with Christian ideals of fasting and prayer. Now in the times when secularism is dominant again, the overshadowing of the New Year's Eve countdown in Times Square and the revelries afterward, continue to interfere with the crazy notion of going to *church* on New Year's Day.

I never heard the word again, *holydayofobligation,* not for two decades, anyway, when I entered the Catholic Church on my own two feet and said "yes" to God-knows-what.

The official collection of holy days of obligation has waxed and waned over the centuries, and even in the years since I became a Catholic. The obligation of declared holy days is to attend Mass and abstain from "servile work," as the *Catholic Encyclopedia* phrases it. In the 1600s, Pope Urban VIII reduced the number of holy days of obligation to thirty-four, in addition to all Sundays. This resulted in close to a day "off" per week, and the beginning of the idea of a weekend. However, noting the high cost of living and the necessity of working the fields and orchards required of agrarian society, Pope Pius X in 1911 confined such days to eight plus Sundays. These days as fixed by Pius were: Christmas (December 25), the Feast of the Circumcision (January 1), Epiphany (January 6), Ascension (forty days after Easter), Immaculate

Conception (December 8), Assumption of the Blessed Virgin (August 15), the feast of SS. Peter and Paul (June 29), and All Saints (November 1).

Feasts that fell from his obligatory list included three that generated large celebrations, particularly in Europe — Feast of St. Joseph (March 19), which is particularly beloved in Italy and cities with large Italian populations; the Nativity of St. John the Baptist (June 24), and Corpus Christi, the Feast that celebrates the Body and Blood of Christ. With each one lost to "obligation," there is a corresponding loss of celebration and memory, individual days becoming collective cultural history. As an example, Bishop Donald Wuerl recollects, "one of the beautiful celebrations I recall from my student days is held on Corpus Christi . . . "

> *In a tradition that goes back to 1778, one of the principal streets of this community is covered with flower petals depicting artful designs and religious scenes. It gives the impression of a carpet of tapestries. People work with great care and skill to cover the entire roadway, so that on the feast of the Body and Blood of Our Lord, the Blessed Sacrament can be carried from one church to another along this "avenue of flowers."*
>
> *. . . I have experienced the joy of carrying the Blessed Sacrament along this beautifully designed and colorful carpet representing the faith, love and devotion of the people . . .*[1]

Gone, those memories stop and do not rebuild or repeat as the days of obligation drop them off like petals on a fading flower. The Solemnity of St. Joseph is subdued and de-obligated, as it nearly always takes place during Lent, although my husband's Italian family members still make the *zeppole* pastries and the St. Joseph novena for the March 19 date. Corpus Christi became the Sunday after Trinity Sunday.

In the United States at least, the Epiphany and the feasts of SS. Peter and Paul dropped away as well. Epiphany moved to the nearest Sunday before or after January 6, and SS. Peter and Paul stayed with June 29, but without the mandatory part. By the time I joined up, the *holydaysofobligation* chant was down to six.

The holy days of obligation are as much a celebration of memories of us as Catholics being set apart in order to come together as they are about theology or living biblical history. Ascension is one such memory-embedded feast day for me and probably always will be.

Forty days after I became a Catholic at that long Easter Vigil, I had my opportunity to experience *real* Catholicism. The Sunday church bulletin reminded "the faithful" of the Mass schedule coming up for the Solemnity of Our Lord's Ascension on Thursday, and that it was a holy day of obligation. That mysterious chant again! Only now I could see what it was composed of, the individual words and how they were assembled. And now the "holy day" was showing me a specific face — Ascension, which I knew in biblical concept as a Protestant, but never knew as a celebration. . . . *as they were looking on, Jesus was lifted up and a cloud took him from their sight.*[2]

I like celebration. I like meeting my obligations, at least if I know what they are. And here it was spelled out for me: *here's the Mass schedule; this is what the faithful do.* It felt so Catholic, and therefore so special, to hurry off to Mass on what looked like an ordinary Thursday night on the outside of it.

But inside, it was special. It was the Ascension. And suddenly this night that was just an ordinary night was rich in memory and purpose. An old biblical story — just one line in the entire Bible! — came to live among us again.

At the intercession prayer, two readers stood and read the names of the dead, all those who had been buried from that church in the past year. It was a large parish and there were many names. I was new and didn't know any of the names. But the church was new too, built with a large arched ceiling, and the sounds of the names echoed as they reached the arch.

When they finished, the readers opened the intercessions up to the congregation and our beloved dead. All around me, the names of people were spoken aloud, murmured, or whispered — names of much-loved people, still loved or re-membered, but beyond our sight or touch. The names floated on whispers to the middle of the church and then rose heav-enward up that arch into the ceiling above the altar. Our dead were no longer forgotten. You could hear, and practically see, those much-loved names, like prayers, gather together and ascend, and it really brought the meaning of the day home to me.

For an acquired Catholic like myself, some of the best holy days of obligation are the Marian ones, like the Assumption of Mary (which I constantly mix up and call "ascension of Mary" — but at least I have the direction, if not the theol-ogy, correct) and the Immaculate Conception. They have no parallel in my old Protestant world, and so they are rich with unfamiliar imagery and obscure (to me) Latin hymns that I can only hum. They make me feel Catholic.

When I was young and growing up in the old mill towns of Rhode Island, I sometimes saw the signs for street fairs or carnivals, put on by churches as part of the Feast of the Assumption of Mary. I thought it must be great to belong to a church that could encourage your attendance with hot dogs and stomach-turning rides and throwing up your hot dogs. The few Catholics I knew who also went to those festivals always seemed to be talking about the throwing up part.

It sounded glamorous to me.

On the other hand, I never heard a word about the Immaculate Conception until one of those pesky church bulletin reminders let me know the Mass times for this *holydayofobligation.* Less than three weeks before *Christmas?* Are you *kidding?*

But being a convert doesn't make me special in my ignorance of this particular obligation. There are a *lot* of people who don't know what this feast is, and as a result, I can nearly guarantee, anywhere in the Catholic world, what the homily for December 8 will be. The priest will get up and look at his expectant congregation, sigh deeply, and then say, "The Immaculate Conception is *not* a feast about the virgin birth. It's a feast of Mary, and how she was conceived without original sin, to prepare her for the arrival of our savior."

And then we are led down truly difficult pathways of doctrine and tradition that brace this belief. But by then, half the congregation is mentally reviewing the status of their Christmas shopping, and the other half is wondering where those great days of Latin hymns have gone. This feast became a holy day of obligation in 1854, but it clearly needs some good memories and a few traditions, and maybe a little dancing in the streets and throwing up hot dogs to make it live for generations to come.

I have a prayer I wrote in my prayer journal for December 8, 2001, quite unlike any other composed for the Feast of the Immaculate Conception: *Today we renew our wedding vows, touched by a Marian whisper,* Stay close to each other. *Our vows fill in the spaces between the words and make us one.*

Felix and I married years before my conversion in a ceremony validated by the Episcopal Church and the Commonwealth of Massachusetts. He was willing to visit church for marriage; he was not willing to follow me into Catholicism.

The years passed, and like so many things you commit to without knowing what you're getting into, we learned and deepened and scraped and struggled into a real marriage, the sacrament of being church together what we were not as individuals. Eighteen years of marriage said what my original vows had not: This is a good man, a man more Christian in the world than most who proclaim such a faith, a man who bangs on his elderly neighbors' doors and says, you all right? You need me to do something? And the ones too embarrassed to call for help accept help when it bangs on the door like a vigorous angel and demands to assist. Christ has been that to me in my life; Felix is that to our neighbors. Let us re-vow, I thought, now that we know what our vows look like, and acknowledge the truth of what we vowed in our youthful ignorance.

To my surprise, he agreed to it. I had been to Mass at a tiny little church pressed against the Pacific on the Big Island of Hawaii. This church had no doors, was always open to the world, and the priest would always offer to renew wedding vows under the coconut trees outside after Mass.

Better than a postcard souvenir, I thought, and, assuming a small donation would be welcomed, what a charming way to keep a small parish in some pocket money.

I read up on the sacrament of marriage and told Felix what I'd been reading. I practically gave little homilies from the Letters of St. Paul: *For the unbelieving husband is made holy through his wife,* Paul had written.[3] "You don't want me to do all the heavy lifting, right? It's about us, together, that makes us church."

Finally, Felix said, "Are you proposing to me?"

"I am. It's my turn. Please consider my request."

He did, and unprompted, came back one evening and said, "Okay."

I looked at the dates of our trip to Hawaii. I wanted a date I could remember, like our wedding anniversary, one that could acquire a patina of aged memory over time. December 8 stood there on the calendar.

"It's either that or the attack on Pearl Harbor," I said. He went with Mary's day of singular grace.

Well, first of all, this time it wasn't Boston, and renewal of vows would be quite different memories. It was the same old Felix, of course, in his morning shower, singing, "Going to the chapel, and I'm gonna get ma-a-ah-ried. . . . " He carefully dressed for the occasion in white golf shirt and black golf shorts, "like a tuxedo," he explained. And then, because it was the same old Carol, he looked me over head-to-toe before he finally said, "Are you really going to wear those flippies to my wedding?"

It was the Feast of the Immaculate Conception even here, on a bit of land in the middle of the sea. The tiny church filled quickly. There was only room for twenty to sit, and then you're spilled outdoors to the coconut trees. Father O'Brien donned his liturgical stole over his aloha shirt and a double maile lei, and processed quickly to the front. His dog dropped down for a nap nearby.

The readings were a striking blend of Adam and Eve name-calling and Angel Gabriel and Mary singing their headline news. Felix looked puzzled, but he was obviously trying to stay with it, which was nice. Father O'Brien delivered the

homily, my prewedding-vow homily as it were. Either the dog
sighed in his sleep or the priest did in his little pulpit before
beginning: "Today is the Feast of the Immaculate Conception.
The Immaculate Conception doesn't refer to the virgin birth.
It means that Mary was conceived without original sin... "

It must get sent to all the priests right after Thanksgiving.
Explain this. Nobody gets this...

I thought about Boston, about eighteen years together. Out
of the corner of my eye, I saw Felix watching the waves rolling
in beyond the church.

After Mass, Father O'Brien shook everybody's hand and
then returned to us at the altar. The dog's hopes for escape
dashed, he stood watch in the doorless entry while Father
O'Brien hauled out a separate book and began...

Dearly beloved...

I choked on the memory, and Felix's eyes looked a little sus-
piciously red. For some reason, I thought the vows for renewal
might say something different, bind us to new and improved
lives together, as a detergent ad might claim. Instead, once
again, we told each other we would love, honor, obey, cherish.

Those are hard words when you begin to understand them.
Mary's position of immaculate conception is an enormity I
can't begin to understand, but I celebrate it out of respect and
wait for the fun part of the celebration to begin. Marriage was
something we took on for the fun part and then grew into its
meaning.

These words we said — and we were barely able to speak
them in our emotions — meant so much more after eighteen
years. We owned the knowledge of riches and the concerns
of poorness together now. We knew what those words look
like. We had taken health for granted as well as "for better,"

and we had tasted illnesses, deaths, and "for worse," too. The words resonated with meanings drawn from life.

"Persevere," said Father O'Brien when we were done. "Without that, you have nothing." He pulled the double lei from around his neck and draped one end around me and one around Felix, intertwining us both in fragrant maile leaves.

And then he removed his stole, and he and his dog roared off in a truck.

This feast day of obligation resonates now, tied as it is to memories of the sacrament and obligations of marriage. *We're together, Hail Mary. How are we doing? And how are you this year?*

Memories and obligations are how holy days of obligation are woven to tie us to our faith. I learned that from my mother-in-law.

"What time is it?" she would ask during our visits.

"It's 4:00 p.m."

She needed to know. She had already lost dimensions through near-deafness and poor eyesight, and by her ninety-second year, the fourth dimension, time itself, seemed to be on "stuck." Ann had been granted the gift of a long life and had never really opened the package. Now it was too late for anything but questions.

"What time is it *now*?"

"It's 4:10 p.m."

"That's all? I thought it was *much* later than that!"

Poor Ann. She couldn't see the clock or hear it chime, and for something so empty, time hung heavy around her neck. She'd been impatient and anxious her whole, long life. She was impatient for death's knock on the door. She's never waited this long for anything in her life. She was afraid she wouldn't hear the knock when it came.

But as Jesus himself said after his resurrection, and before his ascension into heaven, *it is not for you to know the times or the seasons. . . .*[4] Ann didn't know when or how. We didn't know either. I prayed many prayers for her as if her soul had already departed. There were days I wasn't quite sure which side of heaven and earth she was facing.

Came Ascension again, that lovely, bittersweet memorial, when the dead you so dearly loved get to visit at least, but never stay, when those names are remembered and whispered until they float together into the rafters of the church.

"There's another way to look at it," said Father Don crisply. The whispered names of memory stopped for a moment. I was still trying to decide where Ann belonged this particular Ascension.

"Think of the large, beautiful sailboat that carries away our dead," he continued. "We stand on the shore and watch the sails until we can no longer see them against the horizon. And then we turn away. *She's really gone,* we say, and leave the shore full of loss and sadness."

Yes, Ann, I thought. She's stepped on that boat now, but I can still see her.

"But there's another shore," Father Don said. "On the other side of the horizon, they have been waiting. *Here it comes!* they say. And the sails grow larger again against the new horizon as the boat comes closer to those who have been awaiting its arrival at long last."

Like Pete, Ann's husband, who died three years before her. He promised to go last, to watch over her to the very end, and he probably hung on longer than humanly possible with his emphysema and lung cancer, but came up a few years short of his promise. Yes, he would be there saying, *What took you so long?* And Ann would say, *Well, I didn't know what time it was.*

We went back to see her four days after Ascension. She was in the hospital, having suffered a minor heart attack perhaps. They weren't sure. She wasn't quite with us when we got there, but she wasn't fighting against us either.

"Time's getting short," she said.

The hairs on my arm stood up. That wasn't her usual way. I wanted a happy ending now, a reconciliation of a long life, recognition of the possibilities ahead, *anything.*

"What time is it?" she asked.

"It's 2:30, Ma," Felix said. "We got here as fast as we could."

"Maybe that's *your* time," she said. "Not mine."

I wanted a happy ending. But when she'd had her say, I knew it wasn't about what I wanted after all. And they were waiting on that other shore for the ship that had just made sail.

Ascension now had its obligation of memory in the departure of her ship and all the others who had boarded that ship, the time when we recognize their journey to the other shore.

There is a problem with these lovely tokens of Catholic obligations, however: they're melting.

"You're writing about the holy days of obligation?" one of my fellow Benedictine oblates asked. "Write fast before they're all gone." At the diocesan level, for reasons of pastoral concern, bishops may request lifting some obligations from the calendar. Whenever January 1 (Solemnity of Mary, Mother of God), Assumption, or All Saints falls on a Saturday or Monday, the obligation to attend is removed. One has to assume that going to Mass two days in a row is more than most of the flock can bear. The obligation of January 1 has been dispensed in the Los Angeles diocese completely. Is the old rowdy secular celebration overshadowing the feast day for good?

Pope Pius X may have intended to give uniformity out of his grand list of special days for Catholics, but in the United States, the uniformity is largely mystical.

"Let me tell you my Ascension Thursday story," a friend from the east e-mails. "We were out in Chicago for our big-time trade show, which was crawling with Catholics. So, of course, there was Mass on Thursday afternoon. Even though the other Catholic in my group declined to attend, I made my way to the St. Charles Ballroom and promised to meet my non-attending colleagues for drinks after Mass. Imagine my dismay when the priest announced that in the Archdiocese of Chicago, Ascension Thursday is no longer a holy day of obligation. I confess I considered slipping out but I STAYED UNTIL THE END. How was *your* Ascension Thursday?"

The official chant, the sanctioned-off *holydaysofobligation,* may be lessening, but there is no reason why we Catholics cannot set apart days of our own choice and make them holy. St. Thomas More, I am told by a Benedictine monk, made Thursday his holy day because his Sunday held too many official duties to honor as sacred.

"Happy Feast of St. Benedict!" shouts Father Ron's e-mail when I arrive at work on July 11. "I hope it is a day filled with blessings and graces for your Benedictine spirit."

Since I am a Benedictine oblate, and since my abbot, the oblate-master, continues to invite us all to show up at the abbey for Mass and lunch, and since I have shown up every year since becoming an oblate, it has become my holy day of obligation.

On July 11 I *should* be at a regional comprehensive planning meeting, a group where I hold an elected position representing stakeholders in the future growth of the county. I *might* have enjoyed a professional meeting scheduled for July 11 whose agenda calls for recognizing lobbyists into the professional communicators' organization. But I *choose* to be with Benedict and the others who will choose to be with him on this day.

"Happy day!" my friend back east e-mails. "Are you at the abbey? I hope you are having a lovely day. You are probably sitting at Mass, playing with e-mail on your PDA."

How does she know? "It is lovely here," I e-mail back (before Mass begins). "This is my holy day of optional obligation. I am waiting for the bells to begin."

I barely tap that out between my roving thumbs when the abbey bells start clamoring for my attention. They have stone hearts, a nearly toneless clanking, and I have always described their feast-day uproar as busting out of those stone hearts. But it is more like *my* stone heart that is busting out, like the promise that the prophet Ezekiel gave from God to replace my stone heart with a flesh heart.[5] The novena I have prayed for St. Benedict's feast day is in its ninth day. "Let us rejoice in the Lord," the antiphon begins for this day, "celebrating the memory of the holy abbot Benedict!"

Benedict waits for us to arrive this day, like an adoring parent whose far-flung children, ranging from the dutiful to the derelict, show up for the obligatory holiday dinner. We are all his, Sweet Ben's children. He uses his feast to gather us all in, his family, the way we once were gathered up in our family gatherings of the past, the way we'll someday be "all together again" when we die, as the abbot promises us.

Our holy father Benedict's white ivory statue sits in front of the altar, behind his relic, surrounded by white lilies. The distant children arrive, the living and the dead, the saints, the wanna-bes, and the never-wills. Sweet Ben draws us together.

I am restless and waiting, keep looking around anxiously until I realize that I've been looking for the oblates and monks who have died on my watch. Now why would I be looking around the monastery for them?

Then I look again to the altar, and realize where they are. They are with us, of course, but on the other side of the altar, the other shore. My Benedictine patron Blessed Joanna Mary, St. Benedict himself, my beloved dead, all of them are waiting for the first glimpse of that ship that we watched set sail so sadly.

They are all exactly where they want most to be. And so am I, since holy days of obligation don't set us apart as special, but bring us together in presence and memory.

And someday all of us will be together again.

NINE

The Rule of St. Benedict

IF I ADDED UP all the pounds I've lost, they would total more than most men weigh at their heaviest. Unfortunately, when it comes to body weight, I'm the best, most efficient, lost-and-found department around. What has been lost has also been found. If I add up all the finds, I am twenty pounds net gain.

Some gain. Why do I go through this my whole adult life?

Early in our weight struggles determining how many pounds were hereditary heaviness versus how many pounds came from the ordinary eat-too-much weight, Felix took a business trip to Puerto Rico. At the resort where he stayed one night, a couple caught his eye as they came out of one of the casinos. "They were so happy together," he reported back. "They reminded me of the way we are, ordinary people who are special to each other because they're in love. As soon as I saw them I thought of us and wished you were there with me."

And then, just when the going was good, and I was ready to let out a big "awwh," he added, "They were both roly-poly little chubs, but they didn't seem to care that they'd gone to seed. Do you think we'll ever get like that?"

I threw one shoe at him.

The couple I never saw has stayed before my eyes and his ever since. "Can I go to seed now?" one of us will ask, wistfully standing in front of the chips row at the supermarket, or lingering too long with the pizza ads from the Sunday paper. Is it time?

And the other one, perhaps temporarily the stronger, or just the less hungry or crazy one that day, looks over and says, "Not now. Maybe later."

Is it "later" yet? Why do we do this to ourselves? Food is one of the social and sensual pleasures in life, or it can be if two bags of taco chips consumed at one sitting is discounted from the discussion. ("They were on *sale,* two bags for five dollars. What could I *do?*" protests Felix.) Food is a basic need. Food is a drug if used for the wrong reasons or in excess. Food is food, not a battleground. Why do we make it so?

When we were younger, when we were dating or working our way onto the career ladder, appearances mattered, or at least we felt that they did. We ingested a host of media and marketing messages about how we looked and how others perceived us until those messages became us.

But the truth that we only seemed to learn much later, if ever, was that nobody was paying that much attention to us after all — it was all about them, the way it was all about us. So there we were, stuck with those media-fed, market-driven values of what matters and what doesn't about our appearance, just when appearance becomes harder and harder to maintain.

"If I have to get old and wrinkled, well, fine, but I'm not going to let myself get old and *fat!*" we declare. There are limits. We have our rules. We have drawn our line in the sand, and the battle will continue to rage among our weak natures, our raging appetites, and our gently eased waistlines.

If we're lucky, the eyesight will fade with the willpower. Because otherwise, giving up is what giving in looks like, and that's like saying the game's over, and we've lost.

We have our rules . . . Dieting never works in the long term, we are told. You've got to change your habits and your way of looking at food as well as your way of consuming it. It has to be a way of life, not the exception.

A rule of life in the spiritual sense is the same no-frills, sensible-shoes approach to how we live our faith in the world. I can live in the here-and-now and figure that my heavenly reward will be debatable after I die. Or I can try to live in such a manner that I can at least glimpse heaven in the here-and-now. A spiritual rule is simply a way of living that reminds you of the essentials every day.

Eight years after becoming Roman Catholic, I took beginner vows as a Benedictine oblate. By that, I pledged to follow St. Benedict's Rule to the best of my ability and as my station in life permitted. At the time I said yes to that, it seemed pretty lame and open-ended as promises go. But I was used to making up rules for myself all the time. I called them *resolutions,* and usually bunched them, not around the turn of the calendar year, but around the opening of a new diary.

I was a compulsive diarist as I was compulsive in many areas of my life, and my compulsion had its sick side: I started many, *many* diary volumes, but I had trouble finishing them. Maybe it was a control issue. Maybe it was anxiety, looking too far ahead to see where I was going *next*, while tripping my feet over where I was *now.*

I bought a new diary today. I've been keeping an eye on the pages in this book as I fill them, ticking them off in mental 25-page lots. When I hit page 450, I began to get preoccupied with the next volume and wanted to finish this one off quickly.

Bought a new one to stop the anxieties. The anxieties were just warming up. Should I leave the rest of this volume blank?

Felix suggested I draw X's through the remaining pages. I went one step further and cut out the remaining pages with scissors. It looked like an angry, rage-induced haircut when I was done. I am the sum of the half-digested diary volumes. They are all me. I am my diary.

The other piece of my diary compulsion was the resolutions that accompanied each fresh start. It was like New Year's Day with each volume, as I tacked a fresh round of rules and order onto the written reflection of my life:

I have two criticisms to carry forward into this new diary. To level criticism at a personal diary seems ridiculous, but I do it anyway.

1. *Stop wasting ink writing about how shallow the diary entries are.*

2. *Stop writing about lack of emotion.*

3. *Stop using psychological jargon.*

I lectured myself and resolved myself with every volume's beginning, and absolved myself and dissolved myself as I hacked away abandoned pages at its end. As anybody knows who has tried to alter a lifestyle habit like smoking or swearing, it is easier to substitute (good habit for bad) than to remove. The smoker substitutes carrot sticks for the oral fix; the ex-drinker shows up at support groups instead of the local bar. For me, substituting for my diary demons created its own rules, some quite elaborate and superficial.

There was the diary I set up with a "color scheme" that I had to index in the front of the book to keep it all straight in my mind: writing exercises were highlighted in wavy green pen; "snapshots" (artistic images I might use someday) were highlighted in purple; writing ideas or germs of ideas were outlined in black, writing drafts were written in blue; poems were written out in orange felt-tip pen; dreams were in brown; submissions and rejections of my writing were noted in red; and *Farmers' Almanac* information was yellow highlighted.

Just keeping myself in the correct color and type of writing implements must have been quite a challenge — was I afraid I wouldn't know a poem I'd written from a *Farmers' Almanac* note on the Full Wolf Moon without distinguishing orange felt-tip from yellow highlighter? And yet I held tightly to my color-coded "rule" for 400 pages of diary. What a relief it must have been to hack out its remaining pages before I finished.

St. Benedict wrote his rule for beginners in the vernacular Latin of the sixth century during a period of external chaos and changing values that has echos for our own times. The little red paperback the old abbot handed me was hardly worth the $6.95 cover price for its diminutive size. It reads at little more than 9,000 words. The standard-size novel will run from 60,000 to 130,000 words.

This little Rule of Benedict of Nursia, modeled after a longer, more stringent rule written by someone known only to us as the Master, legislates behavior for those who choose to follow it. It gives guidelines for prayer, silence, work, obedience, and even clothing, drinking, and eating. (Where was this book in my collection of diet books, huh?) But more important to Benedict than how or why things are ordered the way they are, is the motivation behind the observance.[1]

When I stumbled into the Benedictines, the first thing the abbot did was feed me. Once that kind of nourishment was satisfied, he handed me a little red paperback with the title, "The Rule of St. Benedict" on it and asked innocently, "Do you like to read?"

And of such incidental, nearly accidental, encounters are lives changed.

A few months later, I stood with two other individuals in the monastery's retreat chapel and said to myself, *sure I'll try this for a year and see what happens.* The novitiate vow gives more dignity to my "try before you buy" mentality, and it *did* say the vow was renewable every year, which was great in case I didn't like it. I didn't know what a "rule" was at that moment, and certainly didn't know there were other spiritual rules available to choose from, or that you could find your own rule of life from the scriptures or make up one the way I seemed to with diaries. The only problem with making up my own was that I changed the rules as fast as I made them. A real spiritual rule doesn't bend just because I do.

Take a scriptural rule as an example of a clear way of life. In his letter to the Romans (chapters 12–13), Paul spells out a way of life with PowerPoint clarity: love one another, contribute to the needs of the holy ones, pay your taxes (!), owe nothing, and don't look for revenge. In the forty-four verses that constitute those two chapters are everything you need to live a Christ-centered life, if you can remember them all every day. Before I became a Benedictine, there was an entire year that I wrote every day in my prayer journal: *Rejoice in hope, endure in affliction, persevere in prayer*[2] as a sort of mantra/rule. If I could have found a rule of life that fit on a tee shirt or bumper sticker, I might have chosen that. I was looking for how to live my Catholic life on a daily, lifestyle basis. I didn't think covering the house with statues of saints and madonnas would do it. I thought there must be rules out there that a real Catholic knew about, and I did not. And for all my looking, I was found. I was given a rule, courtesy of Benedict, through his ambassador, a retired abbot. Unlike Catholicism, which I chose, the Rule of Benedict chose me.

Indeed, there *are* other rules of life, I learned, years after I pledged away my option to Benedict. One of the oldest came from St. Augustine, written about the year 400, which promotes prayer, moderation, self-denial, and chastity. The Franciscan and Dominican orders have distinct ways of life written by their founders, as do the Carmelites and others.

Nor are all such rules part of the distant, dusty past, lopsidedly applied to our world and our life. As recently as 1985, The Order of Julian of Norwich — a contemplative, semi-enclosed order of the Episcopal Church — was founded. Their rule is based on St. Benedict's, with an additional, strong Carmelite ethos of silence and solitude.

There are many other rules of life to live by, but the one I was given was one of the most venerable and followed, not only by monastics, but by laypeople exactly like me who wanted a way to follow in their world.

Why follow a rule at all? Surely the church has enough do's and don'ts to keep me busy for a very long time. Why add the unnecessary, unrequired act of following a rule of life as well? And why does following this particular Rule of St. Benedict keep me Catholic?

I think for me, product of the late 1960s/early 1970s culture, there is a sense of needing order and structure, a rule for my unruly soul. Put in a more positive light, what I want is freedom. And following a rule frees me in many ways. I have survived the shaping times of the anything-goes sixties only to arrive at middle age in the third millennium, a time like Benedict's of great chaos, vanishing values, and an unstable environment for my quest for stability. And, having sought out and desired Catholicism for whatever reasons brought me in, I am now looking for the reasons to stay.

"Perhaps what I'm looking for," says a traditional Catholic woman in a middle management position, "is more rules, some guidance that I'm living my life the way it should be lived or, you know, helpful hints, or how should it be improved? What should I be doing? . . . I just feel like I need some more guidance."[3]

In a world rich in choice and ripe in opportunity, my way has not had the results I've been hoping for. My way has veered between "more" and "how much do you want for that?" Even Catholicism, this lovely bulwark of the faithful for so many hundreds of years, is talking like the political parties I work with as a lobbyist: liberal views, conservative actions, advocacy on a host of political issues, etc.

Where's God in all of this?

I need a road map. I get lost and distracted too easily.

"The Rule has ecumenical appeal for those who feel a longing for an often undefined something more," says one writer.[4] I want "more" but it isn't the "more" I once looked for in alcohol, nicotine, food, or even religious gift stores. I want more clarity. I want more simplicity. I want more God in my life. I want less me in it.

"Why do you make the golf team sign a personal behavior contract?" I asked my university's golf coach. "Is that standard? Do you wish you had done it when you played college golf? Why do the students even sign it?"

"They need to be accountable for their actions," says Fred. "At age eighteen, most of them have no clue about the commitment necessary to be successful at anything. They have all achieved small levels of success or they wouldn't be here. But to transition from being a child to being an adult is a long and trying process."

Right: like trying to get from spiritual brat to at least adolescence. I got this far: now what?

Fred makes his students sign a one-page contract that Benedict would have liked. It covers practice commitments, grade expectations, dress guidelines, and attitudes regarding team play — plus the punishments for breaking the rules, which look like athletic versions of penance and excommunication to me. He put his rule together for his players because, as a college player, he didn't have goals and guidelines set up for him. "It was my fault," he says, "because I don't trust a lot of people and there wasn't someone to be my teacher for the life side of golf. My players, if they stay the full time, don't have to worry because I am around or I can put them in touch with someone who can lead them."

But what's the student's motivation for following the rule their coach has laid down? He has hindsight and a fair amount of hard-earned wisdom. They are eighteen and full of themselves, and think coaching is about perfecting an already perfect golf swing. Do they follow his rule to meet the goals they have already set themselves?

"Hell, no," says Fred. "They don't have a goal, or the goal isn't specific, or they don't realize what it takes to be consistently successful. It's not that simple."

"Then why do they bother with you?" Fred is half the age of the abbot, but I am suddenly reminded of that innocent question — "Do you like to read?" — and the book he thrust in my hands. Why did I bother to read it?

"They do it because, ultimately, they know graduating is important, even if they don't know why," he says. "They think I might know a little bit — *just* a little bit — about what it takes to get better. So they sign on. Some of them stick with the rules and find out that most of what they need to learn isn't taught through swing analysis. A lot don't stick it out and don't learn. By getting good at other aspects of life, you get good at golf. I kind of sneak that one in on them."

Signing a contract means a student has taken a big first step in the long road to success. From learning as he goes along what it takes or doesn't take to be successful — a hit-or-miss process at best — those students front-load the information. You will...you won't...the price of non-compliance...and they sign it, say yes, put me in there for the long haul, I'm your guy, and even if I fail, I'll pay the price and stay the course.

Imagine if God had such a contract. Who would sign it?

Well, my church says God does, and it's called baptism. Somebody else signed for me. I was only two months old. I refused to claim their promises as mine for a long time, even in confirmation class, even having been confirmed twice.

Signing up for the Rule, I didn't put much more thought into it than the confirmations. But once I got in and read the fine print, it said, *this thing's about stability, Buster.*

Uh-oh.

Unique in their vows, Benedictines pledge stability, and Benedict's tools of good works, like my little kit of "keeping Catholic" tools, are practiced "within the stability of the community."[5] Stability means I belong to the oblate community, that I have committed myself to the ongoing search for God within a particular group, that I will not seek to find God "better" elsewhere, that there is no place to go but here.

I'm stuck here. Can I go to seed now?

"Stability says we will walk the major roads of life until the end, no matter what," writes Benedictine nun Joan Chittister.[6]

Stuck! I didn't know that was part of the deal, I have no staying power, it gets boring and stupid after a while, and what if this isn't me, and the real me is waiting in the next available option I try?

It's me now. At least until the next feast of Christ the King, the last week of the liturgical year, like December 31 in the secular calendar. That's when I took my Benedictine vows. That's when I renew them every year. I not only signed up for Benedict's Rule and pledged stability to the place that took me in, but I get to repeat it once a year, every year for the rest of my life. The Benedictines are tidy, however. When I die, they ask: could somebody send back my oblation paper? Then they can close my file. But not until then.

This seems to be quite the irony for the poor woman who color-ink coded her diaries and scissored out the last pages because she never finished them and couldn't bear to witness their blank white testimony to her unfaithfulness.

No problem with that now. You're in. You signed on the dotted line. You promised. You promised GOD.

Does that mean I have to stay Catholic too? What if I don't want to? What if the church makes me crazy, which it seems to do with stunning regularity because I'm delicate in my feelings. What about then?

Those damned golfer kids and their crazy coach Fred have that one sewed up too. He's got students ready to bail all the time. It isn't their fault either. The university changes graduation requirements, they get a faculty member who won't do a make-up exam when they're scheduled to play a tournament on the same day, their playing competitor annoyed them and they threw a club and now Fred's slapping around the penalty clauses like hockey pucks, and who needs this anyway?

"The rules don't mean anything until it gets hard," says Fred. "That's when you get the final grade — who stays with it when it's hard, who bails and finds something else to follow for a while. But it's only for a while. Because if they bail when it's hard, they haven't learned a thing about the rules in the first place."

Will I do it? Will I stay the course and follow the Rule to the best of my ability and as my station in life permits? Maybe someday an envelope will arrive at the monastery. In it will be a single sheet of paper, a bad Xerox copy of something called "Final Oblation," dated November 21, 1999, that the abbot signed firmly, and I in innocent wonder, that called us to my intention to follow the Rule. And whoever is on mail call, whoever has oblate responsibility, will match the name to a folder and block it out with a big X.

That will be proof of my *final* Final Oblation. That will show that I stayed to the last page.

Broken Heart

IT WAS A PERPLEXING, delightful treat to spend four days at a desert hideaway with fifty writers. The delight came, as it frequently does, from finding your people, your tribe: *you're like me, where have you been, and don't ever leave me again.* Writers, particularly, have to work at finding their tribe. It's the nature of their craft and calling that it is done alone. And so there is such delight in spending four days with others who have also crawled out of that alone space to blink and stretch in the mild winter desert sun.

The perplexing part came from the adjective: *Catholic* writers. The retreat was advertised and presumably responded to as a retreat for Catholic writers. I had responded; I was eligible, after all. I had written and published a book that was categorized as spirituality/memoir, and I had a second book under contract. Although late to the game, I was Catholic — and had the piece of paper to prove it. So A + B = C ("writer" + "Catholic" = "Catholic-writer"), does it not?

I wasn't entirely sure. I listened intently when people talked about the topics they were writing about. I counted how many nuns and priests were in the writer group. I noted that one feature of the retreat was the option for daily Mass and also reflection. I ran the numbers again: A + B = C ("nuns and priests in attendance" + "daily Mass and reflection" = "elements that make a retreat a *Catholic*-writer retreat"), yes?

But I had never labeled myself so specifically, and writers know that their best work comes exactly from specificity and concreteness of details. I wanted to try the brand label and see if it fit without cutting off my breathing, without too much wiggling — was I a *Catholic* writer? What did that look like beyond the numbers, the option for daily Mass, the nuns and priests in attendance?

Finally, in a moderated group session, I got brave enough to ask the foolish question: "What makes a Catholic writer a CATHOLIC writer? What does it look like?"

By the sudden silence that followed, I wondered if this was one of those areas where, if you had to ask, that was proof enough you weren't one of the gang. *But I've got the paper to prove it, dammit. I picked you guys . . .*

Finally, one of the editors of a Catholic press began to speak, quite lyrically. "This is an incarnational church. Catholic writing is incarnational . . . "

Incarnational . . . It sounded beautiful, like a gold-gilded icon. I liked that. But I have the soul of my father, the CPA. I count things, hold them in my hand, bring them up to the light, and then run the numbers again.

"Okay, fine, I believe that too. But what does 'incarnational' *look* like?"

I was being dense, not getting what was so obvious to born Catholics, *real* Catholic writers. I lost the thread of the discussion that followed, but played with that gold-gilded icon image of the word *incarnational.* I made my own mental list of words: Mother and Child, Magi, Christmas, star, presents.

What the editor was trying to convey about the church was one of the essential characteristics of it, the thing that defines it away from the pantheon of gods and goddesses of other old religions or the body-free, feel-good lack of substance of New-Age practices. The church is incarnational; it is made from substance, and writers should have more appreciation and taste for such a church than most: The Word was made flesh, and dwelt among us, says the Gospel of John's creation story. This is not a religion of handed-down stories and lore and teachings. This is not a belief system of simply trying to be a better person and trying harder. This is a church of body and blood and all the sufferings and joys that the flesh encompasses.

That icon image of incarnation probably came to my mind because I'd only just packed away the Christmas decorations, and Mother and Child portrayals represent a goodly minority of Christmas cards sent to me. It is hard to remember any spiritual moments in the hubbub surrounding the holiday season, but Christmas is nothing if it is not that incarnational thing, the start of that part of our redemption story — the Word was made flesh and dwelt among us.

No longer a prophesy uttered, the Word broke into human history and became us. Why wouldn't God be happier at the top of the organizational chart, garnering praise and song (and the occasional curses) from the bounty of creation? That's what *I'd* do, but, of course, nobody has yet handed me God's job description and said, "So are you up to the challenge?"

The *Catechism of the Catholic Church* answers my questions on the Incarnation in four points. The Incarnation's meanings are:

1. to save us,

2. so that we would know God's love,

3. to be our model of holiness,

4. to make us partakers of the divine nature.[1]

It sounds good enough to me, and Christmas is about happy stuff, and the Mother and Child icons are so beautiful that I can just click my heels and glide on to the next best thing. But honestly, it doesn't touch me or change me, this knowledge. It doesn't make me Catholic or keep me Catholic. I may have to opt out of the next Catholic-writer conference as ineligible because of that incarnational thing.

What does it look like?

My parish priest Father Don stood at Mass on the Solemnity of the Ascension of Jesus, not safely hidden behind the pulpit with his notes, but right there in front of us with his clip-on microphone, exposed to us like some beating heart, and talking from that place of heart.

"You are sending off your loved one at the airport," he said, "not knowing when they will return, or if, despite their promises, they will return. You stand and watch the plane until there's nothing left in the sky, and oh, the long walk back to the car for the longest ride home of your life . . . "

I was the lector that night, so I didn't have my pocketbook, notebook, or pen with me, having locked it all in the back room. I listened to him talk, and lurked in the back of the church after Mass while he shook *every* blasted hand, and then assaulted him with the back of an advertisement for the men's breakfast that I'd scribbled on with a crayon I borrowed from the kid sitting behind me. I had tried to capture the last sentences of the homily, but they didn't quite sound like him. Father Don agreed, not quite him, went back to his office, and found his text. What he had said to us was: "Ascension is not a sad day. The Lord is not gone from us. I think I see him, my greatest love, in you."

This crazy guy, this priest, is declaring his heart for Christ, and you know what? He says that heart looks like us. What a crazy, incarnational idea that is. What will this church come up with next?

The capital-I Incarnation is a gold-gilded icon of Mother and Child, but this incarnate church makes its bodily claims on pain and suffering as well. Barely three months beyond packing up the Christmas memories, the liturgical year brings us to the heart of *that* heart of the man named Jesus. *The greatest love,* he said, *lays down his life for another. I'll go first.* Experiencing all the sufferings a human could: anticipatory fear, betrayal, torture, mockery, abandonment, and finally a slow death, Jesus showed a heart we will never be worthy of, but can always be grateful for. But its message, its incarnational nature of a heart beating with love, is still our message for today. "It's an incarnational church," the Catholic-press editor said.

Fine. I believe that too. *But what does it look like?* You show me yours, and I'll show you mine.

Maybe once it was represented by the icon of the Sacred Heart. The image of Jesus as "human-hearted" was given in a series of visions to a French nun named Margaret Mary Alacoque in the 1670s. The blue-eyed, blond-haired Jesus exposed a heart of flesh in flames surrounded by a band of thorns and dripping blood from its wounds. This iconography, I am told, was as common in Catholic homes the first half of the twentieth century as the doe-eyed profile of Jesus that graced Protestant homes. Ours may have looked like stills from the Bambi movie, but theirs looked like some bizarreness from another world, "saccharine, kitschy, effeminate, somehow ethereal and grotesque at once," one writer describes it.[2]

Devotion to the Sacred Heart involved quite an elaborate to-do list — personal consecration to the Sacred Heart, observance of an hour of prayer on Thursday night between 11:00 p.m. and midnight as a way to share Christ's sufferings in Gethsemane, reception of Communion on the first Friday of the month as reparation for the indignities inflicted on the sacrament by the indifferent and ungrateful. The stack of corresponding promises reported by Sister Margaret Mary would delight the accountant in me: all the graces necessary to my state of life, peace in my home, comfort in my afflictions, all the way to salvation guaranteed for those First Friday reparations.

Devotion specifically to the Sacred Heart, based on Sister Margaret Mary's visions and images of thorn-encrusted, fiery hearts, is no longer a big part of Catholic life now. It has been dismissed by some for its superstitious overtones, $A + B = C$ ("holy hour" + "Communion on First Friday of month" = "salvation, guaranteed, or your money back"), and masochistic for its suffering-for-Jesus mentality. Where the imagery once served to open the hearts of the faithful to a more compassionate view of God, it is now embarrassingly politically incorrect and certainly unlovable. The trappings of Sister Margaret Mary's image of the Sacred Heart of Jesus have not carried well into the end of the twentieth century and beyond.

For me, this incarnational church in Christ has more the look of a broken heart.

My oblate friend Nancy exposed the broken heart of Christ to me. Nancy was the kind of person who took all the worst oblate jobs for herself. She'd set up all the chairs for the oblate meeting while people like me hung around the abbot talking about lofty stuff. She took the chairs down afterward while the people like me wandered over to the reception area and complained that the goodies weren't laid out yet. That was because Nancy wasn't there yet because she was still breaking down the chairs. She dusted the oblate library and put back our returned books. She mailed out the oblate letter each month. Probably one of the worst jobs was the one she did the best. She sought out all the stray-sheep oblates, the ones like me who didn't know anybody or possess the social skills to mingle, and dragged us back into the fold. "Have you met Laura? She's a writer too. You and Catherine both live in Lake San Marcos. You could ride over here together. Before I put this book back in the oblate library, Carol, you should ask John what he thought of it, and maybe you could borrow it next."

She never asked for help and she rarely got it. "I'm a Martha," she'd say cheerfully. "I have to be doing things." Then she'd push me at the old abbot. "Go talk to him. You do that best. He likes talking to you. You're such a Mary."

The *very* worst job, the one you could only entrust to the one who would never let you down, was still waiting to be done. On the day when we watched the monks bury Father Stanislaus on the canyon top above the Pacific, Nancy and I sat in the rec hall afterward, eating deviled eggs and crying over Father Stanislaus. That was the day I made her promise to take the worst job.

"When it's the abbot's turn, you have to call me," I told her. The monks will be so happy for him that they'll be running all over here clicking their heels, and they'll put up a note about him and that will be it. You'll know because you come here every day and do stuff and they tell you things. I won't know. They won't call all the oblates the way the abbot would. There are too many of us. Nobody loves us the way he does. You have to find me and tell me."

Nancy took my business card with my cell phone, office phone, home phone, mother's phone back east, and Felix's business number all written or printed in. "It will be okay," she said, "when the time comes. We'll know what to do. The abbot won't fail us."

"I know he wouldn't. But it's when *he* dies. It's the others who won't tell us. I'll be in Sacramento or Washington, D.C. I won't know until it's too late. You have to promise you'll find me and tell me."

She looked at the card again and then put it in her wallet behind a prayer card. "I promise," she said slowly. "I don't want to even *think* about him gone — " her eyes got red, "but I'll find you and tell you."

I was as comforted as a child. To know Nancy is to know a doer. If she promises to do a thing, that thing is as good as done.

When I came into the house from work after a particularly good day, I was ready to share my successes with Felix, who did not seem ready to hear them.

"Your oblate friend, Nancy, the one you see at the monastery . . . " he said.

"I know Nancy. What's up?"

"I got a sad call today . . . "

My little work triumphs fled the scene. After all these years it could hardly be a surprise when you're talking about a ninety-four-year-old gentleman, but I still wasn't ready for the news. As I began to cry, all I could think was, well, she kept her promise . . . "Abbot Antony — "

"He called, yes," said Felix. "He wanted to be the one to tell you that Nancy died."

The pain hit hard and had edges that made it difficult to breathe. Nancy was in her early fifties and the picture of energetic health. She had gone to the monastery for Mass on Mother's Day and then gone home. At some point, she called

911, and then her daughter. Her daughter was able to say happy Mother's Day and tell her that she loved her. Nancy was dead when rescue showed up five minutes later.

"Such a cheerful soul," the abbot said when he called again later, sounding anything but cheerful himself. Nancy used to say the abbot didn't really hear your confession as much as read your soul. He'd certainly read hers, but she'd left a promise unkept.

I was indignant. "She was supposed to call me when *you* die!" I howled. "Not the other way around. *Now* what am I going to do?"

"Well, you can come to her funeral on Monday," he said. "I will see you there."

We showed up on Monday, a bedraggled lot of straying sheep bumping into each other in our lostness. The monks who were priests celebrated the funeral mass. The monks who were brothers huddled together in their pew. Nancy's family sat together. Some of the oblates sat together, the ones who knew how to be together in their grief. Nancy's strays were scattered all over the place in solo anguish.

The service went on forever. You didn't want to stay in your pew alone in misery, but you really didn't want to leave her behind at the church or the cemetery either. She was not an alone kind of person the way the stray-sheep oblates were. Finally, the Mass was ended. Before the words of dismissal were spoken, the cantor sang unaccompanied:

> *May the angels lead you into Paradise;*
> *May the martyrs come to welcome you and take you*
> *To the holy city the new and eternal Jerusalem.*
> *May all the saints who have gone before you*
> *Come to welcome you into God's presence.*

The abbot had been most attentive throughout the service. He paid close attention to the casket as Nancy was carried forward at the beginning. He listened deeply to the words of the Mass and to the singers, all in their turn. And now, finally, in this moment of sung contemplation, he leaned back with closed eyes. As the last notes floated to the back of the church, he wiped away tears from his ancient eyes. There it was, the heart of this church, big enough for all of us to crawl inside and be together again, one last time.

This heart, this incarnational church, bleeds and breaks, weeps and suffers. All is not well, and there are times I want to put down my newspaper and give it all up. But where would I go? This is my broken heart too.

I stumbled into this church as a way of saying thanks for a gift given to me. I didn't join for family reasons, for the correctness of its theology or the moral authority of its social agenda. The going got tough. The going always does. I have no staying power. I never had staying power. Benedict says that's all there is really, this stability. "Persevere," said the priest on the island paradise. "Without that, you have nothing." I tried to find tools that would help me stay. I got sulky and looked for reasons to find the next best thing.

The church keeps handing me reasons to leave. Its priorities are politicized, its priesthood grows old and tired, and its future seems irrelevant. But sometimes you stay, if only to keep the body where its heart is. It's an incarnational church, after all.

The bells ring at the monastery to signify the start of Mass. Well, hello, Nancy; hello, Blessed Joanna Mary, and dear Benedict, who kind of got me into this messy old heart business; hello to all my Benedictine buddies and beloved dead across the other side of this common table. Today we sup together with Christ.

At lunch after Mass, Laura walks over. Nancy introduced us to each other as fellow writers, but we never went near each other after that.

Laura is amazed at herself for coming over and sitting down with me. "It is so unlike me," she says, as shy as I am diffident. But when she saw me, she needed to pass along a message, and that need was stronger than her shyness.

"I had a dream," she said, "or maybe I was in prayer when I saw Nancy's face, and it was so clear. She was sitting on a bench outside and beyond her backyard, and she was surrounded by roses."

It sounded so sweetly familiar. Nancy was always hauling her roses and fruits to the monastery for the monks and their visitors to enjoy.

Laura continued, "Nancy turned and spoke to me. I didn't know her very well, not like you and some of the others. I felt like she needed a messenger who wouldn't get in the way of the message. 'Tell them I'm happy,' she said. I thought you might be one of the ones I was supposed to tell."

I was. I needed to know because it somehow fulfilled her promise, although not the way I expected it fulfilled. Sometimes promises are like that — a heart broken, a heart repaired.

E L E V E N

Stability

THERE ARE A LOT of little empty-calorie sugar gods in my life. I may wish it wasn't so, but watch me turn on a dime when pocketbooks, blank notebooks, tote bags, or spiritual "junk" is involved.

We bought a time-share in Palm Springs for thousands of dollars. When the salesperson went to put all our paperwork into a logo tote bag, I said, "If I knew there was a free tote bag included, you'd have had your sale two hours ago."

"She's not kidding," Felix assured her.

Talk about empty gods! At least some people chase money, power, good times, or looking good. My gods look like a new pocketbook. ("Is this one beaded?" asks Felix with a sigh.)

But I am first of all a Christian, by baptism and later by choice, in confirmation. Upon that Body of Christ, I have layered the clothing of Catholicism — in my case, another choice made, and another confirmation. And over that, I have accepted the Benedictine Rule, a way of life that I renew yearly.

Sometimes it seems like too much, and I yearn for a Zen-like simplicity. But then I've had it simple too: a diary, a kitchen table, a pack of cigarettes, and a rapidly drained jug of wine. Simplicity can also become diminishment, settling for less. I am not some seize-the-day kind of person like Felix.

I am more the run-and-hide and wait-until-it's-over sort of person. I should be a perfect candidate for stability.

Benedict took his tools for living the holy life and said to practice with these tools "in the enclosure of the monastery and stability in the community."[1] The enclosure of the monastery is easy to understand as a place when you drive up a steep hill to get there, and once you are there, you are nowhere else. Oblates have their enclosures too — "the place in which I find myself and the people who surround me," as Benedictine writer Esther de Waal says,[2] where the walls are built from the daily prayers of the office and adherence to a Rule.

I find myself Catholic in a place of change. What will it take to turn away from the sugar gods that whip up my interest but do not nourish? Why should I stay put here anyway, and shouldn't I go about finding something a little less controversial *and* old-fashioned than Catholicism?

They taught us substitution in AA — their rules for mine, their language for my "stinkin' thinkin'," a meeting instead of a bar, the phone instead of the bottle. They had lots of tools to keep you sober, and they were tools of the simplest sort because the stakes were so high.

So is salvation. The first substitute I used for AA itself was Catholicism. I didn't convert from my childhood Episcopal church. I converted from drunk. It was a big leap of faith. When I lost family, friends, co-workers, and spiritual gurus through a series of simultaneous deaths, moves, and transfers, I substituted Benedict's rule and an abbot as its guide. And what Benedict says is: now that you're here (and welcome! thanks for coming!), here's the chance to learn the rest of your spiritual lessons in life by staying here.

It is All Souls' Day, and it feels like Homecoming Weekend. For staying put and sticking around, I have had a full weekend of the most joyous company. Yesterday it was all the saints. My own patron, Blessed Joanna Mary, given to me as if by marriage by the abbot when I became a Benedictine, was part of the Communion that also included Benedict, the holy father of our unruly oblates and sometimes unruly monks; St. Joseph — and thanks again for everything you did this year about Felix's work; and of course, Hail Mary, who said yes to God and became Christ's first disciple, and said, with those kind eyes of hers, "You're tough — Rhode Islanders are tough" — and made me another disciple. All of us crowded in Communion yesterday, together in Christ, eating and drinking.

Today, it's all the souls, all the small-*s* saints. When I enter what I *thought* would be the empty little abbey church, it is not empty at all. Along the stair at the base of the altar are photos of the ten deceased monks of the abbey, the ones who persevered to the end and who, undoubtedly, are still persevering. Their names and birth dates into eternal life are carefully noted. The votive candles for each monk are lit, and fallen maple leaves — hard to find sometimes in southern California — have been gathered up and placed about, as these very souls have been gathered into Christ, and yet are placed in our midst today.

The monks filter in for lauds. Some sit in the first pews instead of the choir so they can pray and remember their community. I remember community too: Oblate Nancy, Parent Albert, Grandparents George and Ellen, Eugene and Violet, Felix's parents Peter and Ann, who have no one else to pray for them.

When I'm done here, I'll move down the road to the mission, where they will have a prayer service and then a memorial procession into their historic cemetery that has buried Native Americans from the 1700s all the way to Carol and Felix, birth dates listed, birth dates into eternal life yet to be determined.

"I'll march in the procession," I told the abbot, "on behalf of all souls, including ours, since when we are gone, there will be none to march for us."

"Not true!" he protested. "*I* will march for you!" And I stand corrected: he will certainly march for all of us, from whichever side of the altar he stands.

When I was in elementary school in Pawtucket, Rhode Island, I was very proud of the fact that I was born in El Paso, Texas. I only lived there for the first ten days of my life before my father was discharged from the Air Force and the new family moved back to Rhode Island.

"Don't make a damned Yankee out of her," a neighbor told my mother before we left.

And, of course, they did. There was nothing else I could become, growing up where I did. But every year when our teachers would fill out their various rosters, they would go around the classroom asking each student their place of birth.

"Pawtucket."

"Pawtucket."

"Central Falls." — the town next to Pawtucket.

"Pawtucket."

"El Paso, Texas."

It was pretty exotic stuff in that place and those times, and I was so proud to be born in the largest state in the country, even if I was going to live out my days in the smallest of states.

My mother was the one who had to break the news to me. "Honey, Texas is no longer the largest state in the union."

I looked at her absolutely horrified, she remembers. And then I said, "What did they *do* to it?"

How could you become Catholic — and stay — in that church the way it treats women? the audience member asked me. When I repeated that question to a woman parishioner recently, she looked perplexed. "Did the church do something to women?"

No — no more than something had been "done" to Texas to change its standing. Something new came along. In the case of Texas, it was Alaska. In the Catholic Church's case, it was feminism, combined with times of enormous change in the church that also changed its terms of engagement.

But I never wanted to be a cleric anyway, and really, neither did Jesus. I have never been part of the ruling order — clerical or secular — and neither was Jesus. He turned to his disciples and said, "Follow me," and they did. When I asked Hail Mary to help me, she did, and eventually led me to follow her Son. When Jesus' teachings got tough, many of his disciples left. The Catholic Church gave out tough teachings too and some left, and I began to consider my options. But Peter answered for the rest of us and said, *Lord, you have the words of everlasting life.*[3] And besides, where else would we go?

And then the road itself became a stumbling block, a cross on a hill outside the city where no one would ever want to be. The number who stayed grew precious few, mostly the women, always Hail Mary among them. It was the women who really knew discipleship and staying the course right into their bones. It was the women, the old stories tell us, who were the first witnesses to the gospel of good news, ordinary women who met and recognized the Risen, who went in to honor Jesus and went forth to bring witness to his rising.

Our soul is waiting for the Lord, the psalmist sings. *The Lord is our help and our shield.*[4] Well, here we are, suddenly, all of us inside a psalm. Somehow, somewhere along the way, my fellow seekers and I lost the idea of a soul that waits, the way Hail Mary and the others waited at the foot of the cross, waited in a locked room for the next step of our salvation. We were too self-actualized, too impatient, too goal-oriented to wait within our soul. We put our soul into running shoes and jogged it out of the house and down the street, and forgot to tell it to come back when it got too far away to see home. Our soul waits for no Lord. We hurry off to find him ourselves.

And like the disciples of the risen Lord, we do not recognize him whom we seek. It can't be because our soul is jogging too fast (certainly not *my* soul anyway), but maybe because souls were never meant to jog, but rather to wait.

A waiting soul will know the Lord when he comes. A waiting soul will see him from afar as he comes. The jogger soul passed the Lord on its self-declared circuit many times, but hurried on, unaware. There are times to be met and time to keep running. Surely the Lord — if that was really who we just passed on the road? — would manifest to us as a burning heart, a hushed awareness, a sweet feeling deep inside, and we would know the Lord as soon as our soul could catch its breath.

The jogger soul was busy on its way — so busy it forgot to pack a map.

How will you know you got to your destination without your map? How will you recognize him whom you seek when he comes near? The seeker soul is open to the possibilities. The waiting soul chooses a few tools to anchor itself, and the waiting itself becomes the consecrated life in the Lord. It doesn't come with runner highs or precious silences or scented candles. Alas, it is never to be found for sale in the local religious goods shop. It comes in the waiting, in stability.

Stability in this place where I find myself and those around me — living and dead — is a good call for this last third of my life. After so much hide-and-seeking, all the lost-and-found moments, it's good to be within sight of home once more.

The new ways matter and change how people see the old. They do not necessarily replace the old ways. Here we are, all of us together, on this shore and the next, creating the prayer of the Body of Christ, this Homecoming Weekend of saints and souls. It is an incarnational church. It is my body too.

— All Souls' Day, 2003

Notes

1. Tools of the Trade

1. Peter Steinfels, *A People Adrift: The Crisis of the Roman Catholic Church in America* (New York: Simon & Schuster, 2003), p. 297.

2. *The Psalms: A New Translation from the Hebrew Arranged for Singing to the Psalmody of Joseph Gelineau* (New York/Mahwah, N.J.: Paulist Press, 1963), Psalm 22:2.

3. *The Holy Bible: Old and New Testaments in the King James Version* (Nashville: Thomas Nelson Publishers, 1976), Psalm 23:2.

4. *The New American Bible* (Iowa Falls, Iowa: Catholic World Press, Word Bible Publishers, Inc., 1987). All biblical references (except the Psalms) are from *The New American Bible* unless noted otherwise.

2. Hail Mary

1. Wade Clark Roof, *A Generation of Seekers: The Spiritual Journeys of the Baby Boom Generation* (New York: HarperSanFrancisco, 1993), p. 177.

2. Acts 2:13.

3. Luke 1:46–47. The entire Magnificat encompasses verses 36–55.

4. www.udayton.edu/mary, the International Marian Research Institute.

5. www.cin.org/prayers/litany_loreto.html

6. Bishop Donald W. Wuerl, *The Catholic Way: Faith for Living Today* (New York: Doubleday, 2001), pp. 64–65.

3. The Eucharist

1. Sally Fitzgerald, editor, *Letters of Flannery O'Connor: The Habit of Being* (New York: Vintage Books, 1980), p. 287.

2. Williard F. Jabusch, "The Vanishing Eucharist," *America*, 188, May 12, 2003, p. 12.

3. *The Psalms* 15:8.
4. John 6:54.
5. Matthew 7:4.
6. Wuerl, *The Catholic Way,* p. 169.
7. Ibid., p. 163.
8. Ron Hansen, "Eucharist," in *Signature of Grace* (New York: Dutton, 2000), pp. 96–97.

4. Novenas

1. Wuerl, *The Catholic Way,* p. 349.
2. Barbara Calamari and Sandra DiPasqua, *Novena: The Power of Prayer* (New York: Penguin, 1999), p. 148.
3. Dianne Bergant, on novenas in "Contemporary Catholics on Traditional Devotions," part 6, edited by James Martin, *America,* 188, April 7, 2003, p. 23.
4. Ibid., p. 24.
5. Calamari and DiPasqua, *Novena,* p. 17.
6. 1 Samuel 16:14.
7. Calamari and DiPasqua, *Novena,* p. 89.
8. Fitzgerald, *Letters of Flannery O'Connor,* p. 145.
9. Calamari and DiPasqua, *Novena,* p. x.
10. *The Psalms* 21:15a.

5. The Divine Office

1. Joan Chittister, OSB, *The Rule of Benedict: Insights for the Ages* (New York: Crossroad, 1992), p. 137.
2. Benet Tvedten, OSB, *A Share in the Kingdom: A Commentary on the Rule of St. Benedict for Oblates* (Collegeville, Minn.: Liturgical Press, 1989), p. 4.
3. Luke 1:68–79.
4. Luke 1:46–55.
5. Rita McClain Tybor, "Pray and Work in the Light of Dorothy Day," in *Benedict in the World: Portraits of Monastic Oblates,* ed. Linda Kulzer and Roberta Bondi (Collegeville, Minn.: Liturgical Press, 2002), p 65.
6. Chittister, *The Rule of Benedict,* p. 75.
7. Elizabeth Collier, on the Liturgy of the Hours, in "Contemporary Catholics on Traditional Devotion," *America,* 188, March 17, 2003, p. 11.

6. The Rosary

1. Anthony C. Meisel and M. L. del Mastro, trans., *The Rule of St. Benedict* (New York: Doubleday, 1975), p. 68.
2. Fr. Peter John Cameron, ed., *Magnificat,* May 26, 2003, p. 363.
3. Cindy Wooden, "Rosary Is Powerful Prayer for Peace, Pope Says in Apostolic Letter," *The Southern Cross,* 91, November 19, 2002, p. 2.
4. Fitzgerald, *Letters of Flannery O'Connor,* p. 521.
5. Ibid., p. 582.

7. Adoration

1. Fr. Richard P. McBrien, "Waning Devotions May Be a Sign of Liturgical Health," *National Catholic Reporter,* April 4, 2003, p. 17.
2. Fr. Brian E. Daley, SJ, on Adoration of the Blessed Sacrament, in "Contemporary Catholics on Traditional Devotions," *America,* 188, April 14, 2003, p. 17.
3. *Catechism of the Catholic Church* (New York: Doubleday, 1995), p. 395.
4. *The Holy Bible, Revised Standard Edition* (San Francisco: Ignatius Press, 1966), Psalm 62:1a.
5. *Eucharistic Devotion: Renewing a Timeless Tradition* (Liguori, Mo.: Liguori/Redemptorist Pastoral Publication, 2002), p. 43.
6. Daley, "Contemporary Catholics on Traditional Devotions," p. 17.
7. Carol Zalaski, "The Dark Night of Mother Teresa," *First Things,* 133, May 2003, pp. 24–27.
8. Matthew 26:40.

8. Holy Days of Obligation

1. Wuerl, *The Catholic Way,* p. 168.
2. Acts 1:9.
3. 1 Corinthians 7:14.
4. Acts 1:7.
5. Ezekiel 36:26.

9. The Rule of St. Benedict

1. Esther de Waal, A *Life-Giving Way: A Commentary on the Rule of St. Benedict* (Collegeville, Minn.: Liturgical Press, 1995), p. xv.
2. Romans 12:12.
3. Roof, *A Generation of Seekers,* p. 142.

4. Verna A. Holyhead, SGS, *The Gift of St. Benedict* (Notre Dame, Ind.: Ave Maria Press, 2002), p. 5.

5. Meisel and del Mastro, *The Rule of Benedict*, p. 54.

6. Joan Chittister, OSB, *Wisdom Distilled from the Daily: Living the Rule of St. Benedict Today* (San Francisco: Harper, 1991), p. 152.

10. Broken Heart

1. *Catechism of the Catholic Church*, p. 128.

2. Christopher J. Ruddy, on the Sacred Heart of Jesus, in "Contemporary Catholics on Traditional Devotion," *America*, 188, March 3, 2003, p. 9.

11. Stability

1. Meisel and del Mastro, *The Rule of St. Benedict*, p. 54.

2. De Waal, *A Life-Giving Way*, p. 35.

3. John 6:68.

4. *The Psalms* 32:20.